The
WHY

The
WHY

HEALTHY HABITS FOR AN EPIC LIFE

TEXT AND ILLUSTRATIONS BY

Isabelle Cornish

murdoch books
Sydney | London

Published in 2022 by Murdoch Books, an imprint of Allen & Unwin

Murdoch Books Australia
83 Alexander Street, Crows Nest NSW 2065
Phone: +61 (0)2 8425 0100
murdochbooks.com.au
info@murdochbooks.com.au

Murdoch Books UK
Ormond House, 26–27 Boswell Street,
London WC1N 3JZ
Phone: +44 (0) 20 8785 5995
murdochbooks.co.uk
info@murdochbooks.co.uk

A catalogue record for this
book is available from the
National Library of Australia

A catalogue record for this book is available from the British Library

ISBN 978 1 92235 135 7 Australia
ISBN 978 1 91166 815 2 UK

Cover and text design by Amy Daoud
Typesetting by Susanne Geppert
Back cover photograph © Joe McGaffin
Text on page 41 from 'The Work of Byron Katie'. Reproduced with permission.

Printed and bound in Australia by Griffin Press

We acknowledge that we meet and work on the traditional lands of the Cammeraygal
people of the Eora Nation and pay our respects to their elders past, present and future.

10 9 8 7 6 5 4 3 2 1

The paper in this book is FSC certified.
FSC promotes environmentally responsible,
socially beneficial and economically viable
management of the world's forests.

**This book is a reminder
to fight for the epic life
you deserve!**

TRIGGER WARNING: This text explores past traumas, eating disorders, mental illness and self-harm. If you are concerned about your mental health or that of a loved one, support is available. Contact Lifeline on 13 11 14, Beyond Blue on 1300 22 4636 or The Butterfly Foundation on 1800 33 4673.

A NOTE FROM IZ

Gender binary is a cultural or social construct that wants to put people in one of two boxes: male or female. I believe that this system does not celebrate individual expression, equality and diversity. Non-binary (or genderqueer) people are individuals that don't identify with being male or female, so instead of saying 'she/her/he/him', they often use the pronouns 'them/they/their'. Gender non-conforming and non-binary individuals should be able to express themselves and be accepted without the limitation of gender binary. In this book, you'll come across the terms 'feminine energy' and 'masculine energy', but it's important to note here that feminine energy does not solely belong to a person that identifies as a woman, and masculine energy is not limited to a person that identifies as a man. I support gender variance and all gender identities. I identify as a woman (she/her) so, for the purposes of this book, these are the pronouns I will often use.

~~~~

It all started with a flyer.
Was it the answer to my heart's desire?
Before we dive in and your head starts to spin,
I'd better rewind,
Give you some insight into my mind.
I was born on planet space,
Sent down to join the human race.
I'd rather be dancing naked,
Than at a party wasted.
I love the ocean
And running in motion.
I have ADHD
And a red kelpie named Bee.
I'm a girl that lives by her heart,
Lost in an imaginary art.

~~~~

About Me

I am a woman in my twenties. A tad crazy (as you will be able to tell from reading this book), I live by my heart and have a deep love for health and wellness. Some of you may know me as an actor, influencer or health and wellness kiddo. However, what I value most is living an authentic life in alignment with my heart's desires.

Two of the things that I love most in life are acting and being in nature. When I'm performing, I experience a beautiful flow state where everything around me disappears and I'm wholly absorbed in the moment. I like to think of this state as being in the present – in a zone where everything feels fun, effortless and awesome. This is the feeling I get when I spend time in nature, especially when I'm in the forest or by the ocean.

I grew up in the Hunter Valley in New South Wales, Australia and I have three older brothers and an older sister. My school years were quite rough. During primary school, I was bullied about the shape of my body. I struggled to concentrate, which often led to me getting in trouble. I always felt different and like an outsider. I had not yet learned to love my intricacies.

During my teens, I was lucky to attend a performing arts high school. This school was outstanding for my creative development and growth. However, I have attention deficit hyperactivity disorder (ADHD), so that made the academic side of high school very difficult for me. There were only a select few classes I could concentrate in – sport, music and drama, for example. All I wanted to do was act. I devoted any moment I could to making homemade movies on a small VHS video camera. From age 15, I would skip school any chance I got. I would wait until my mum left for work then run back home from the bus stop.

I was a hurricane during those teenage years. My nights were spent drinking goon (very cheap wine) and my days were spent getting high and taking 5 hours to walk to the McDonald's that was only a couple of hundred metres away. I spent most weekends in my bedroom, tattooing my friends with a tattoo gun that I purchased from eBay. Yep, I know!

As time went on, I was still determined to pursue acting, and my family supported my creativity. But my mum was juggling work and study and couldn't afford to take time off to drive me to Sydney, so I had to wait until I was old enough to get there myself.

When that time came, I'd travel roughly 3 hours each way on the train for one 10-minute audition. My hard work payed off and I began working on different TV shows. Over the next few years, I continued commuting while filming *Dance Academy*, *Rescue Special Ops* and *Home and Away*.

I was 17 when I started on the TV show *Puberty Blues*. A steady job enabled me to move out of my family home to Sydney. On paper, life was good, but inside I started to struggle. Spending my weekends partying in Kings Cross definitely didn't help.

My emotions during this time were so erratic. Some days were amazing, but other times I just felt so flat and down, as if the world was crashing around me. Nothing felt fulfilling. My soul was craving connection, inspiration, nourishment and love. I was on a radical rollercoaster and something needed to change.

It all came to a head one day on set. I was in the hair and makeup trailer and I could barely stop myself from bursting into tears. I felt disconnected, and I had no mindful 'tools' to nourish my crying heart and soul. I just felt an intense emptiness.

So, as I sat there, with a blank journal in front of me, I started to seek answers. All of a sudden, it began to make sense … I needed a deep connection to something. I needed a way of living that would support me throughout life. I needed to upgrade my health, learn to love myself and connect with the natural world around me. I saw a door opening. A clear vision revealed a path of health and wellness.

I often get these visions, as if I am looking deep into my future. I don't know exactly when they started. They happen at random times and come and go in a flash. However, what I see and feel leaves me with an understanding of a clear path forward. These experiences help me to make heart-centred decisions.

I want to go back now to one of these moments, to share with you how I got here, and how you came to be reading this book.

IT ALL STARTED WITH A FLYER ...

One morning in August 2018, I was in my usual stomping ground, adventuring by the sea near Byron Bay on Australia's east coast. I rocked up to the beach in my campervan, laced up my hot pink trainers and got ready to go for a run.

Off I went with my headphones in, feeling the sweet ocean breeze and morning sun on my skin. Everything was in flow until a large flyer came blowing across the path and wrapped itself around my legs. I stopped in my tracks to unpeel this huge poster, thinking

I would just put it the bin. When I turned it over, I saw a multi-coloured psychedelic graphic of a mushroom. The bold letters described a music and arts festival called 'Mushroom Valley'. I peered down at the colourful graphics, showing a rainbow – I was definitely intrigued, but I was also confused.

I didn't know anything about this event, but I was feeling a tingling deep inside my belly – my intuition was trying to tell me something: to take the leap and follow my heart. So, that was it. I left the beach, drove home and instantly purchased a ticket to this Mushroom-Valley-music-festival thing. The festival was a 14-hour drive up the north coast of Australia, but I didn't think twice. I just knew I had to be there. I was following a rainbow.

Rainbows hold huge meaning and purpose in my life. To me, they represent the magic and beauty of this world. I like to view my life as one of chasing the rainbow. It means not settling in a space where I don't feel okay. It means following my dreams and committing to my health and happiness. The rainbow reminds me to always seek growth. It means to always look for opportunities to bring love and light into my life when I lose it. It means following my heart but trying not to fixate on an end goal, where everything is perfect, like a 'pot of gold'. It means staying present, celebrating and being grateful for all the small ways that I show up.

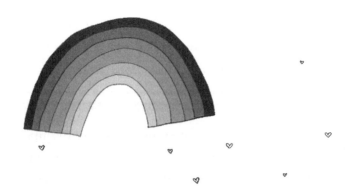

It was a big journey up north, and the very first time I had travelled so far in my campervan. I was thinking, *What the hell is this festival? Why am I going? Will I be all alone?* I was scared, but also excited in knowing that I was living life driven by my heart. I drove across what felt like half of Australia until I was in the middle of nowhere. The land was in a terrible drought, cracked and dry. I spent hours in the car surrounded by bush and dirt, trying to find my way. The suspense was intense, especially after losing mobile phone reception and hitting large cracks in the earth that sent my festival 'bio glitter' (aka biodegradable glitter – way better for the beautiful planet!) and art supplies flying into the air.

~~~

I arrived in a cloud of dust.
Temperatures as hot as balls.
The vibration is as pure as glacier water.
Colours, costumes, campsites.
Bold beats.
Bare feet.

~~~

But, I was in. I set up camp and reached for my oracle cards. These cards, which have been used for centuries, are great for guidance in setting an intention, inspiration or introspection. They come in many styles, but my favourite pack contains 56 butterfly cards, each with a particular message. They offer me a different perspective, help me to navigate life's crossroads and support me when I'm setting an intention for a new experience. I closed my eyes and, guided by my intuition, chose a card. It was the 'Celebration' card – a reminder to take a moment to stop and celebrate. I constantly get caught up striving for the next goal and need a reminder to acknowledge and rejoice in my achievements great or small.

The weekend was everything my mind, body and soul craved. Each day was a journey. The music was transformational and hundreds of us connected with dance, barefoot on Mother Earth. The wellness workshops and Australian bushland offered me a sense of space to heal and rejuvenate. I connected with my roots. There was no mobile phone reception, no showers and I didn't know anyone. I had to practise being my own friend. I fell deep into surrender. I was forced to tune in to my heart – to find love and comfort far away from home.

As the festival came to an end, I was feeling so inspired. I didn't just want to attend these events; I wanted to be a part of them. I think that's the power of putting yourself in the unknown. The workshops sparked a sense of magic inside of me that I'd forgotten about; it had been buried. I realigned with my purpose and I was reminded of my mission to write a book to help others, which has fuelled my fire since I was a teenager. It's the same drive that has propelled me to write for hours in the middle of the night. It's the force that made me start my blog, as well as become a personal trainer, health coach and Jivamukti yoga and meditation teacher. This was the moment that I knew I had to do everything I could to write a book. I had been thinking about it for such a long time. The desire had been held in my heart for years, and it was time to take action.

My determination powered me to drive 14 hours back to Byron Bay in one day. I couldn't stop; my heart was pushing and pulling me towards home so that I could begin. I got inside the door and turned on my computer, searching for as many books and wellness, arts and music festivals as possible. I needed to share! I also needed to make contact with a publisher.

I saw that Wanderlust Festival was about to tour across Australia and I thought I'd try my luck. I sent a few emails and made some calls. Why not? I thought. It seemed like divine timing. Within a week, I had been asked to be a part of Wanderlust Festival, as the MC had just pulled out. I had never hosted anything before, and I was scared shitless. But the adventure didn't stop there.

Fronting Wanderlust led me to reconnect with a nice boy I met in America 6 years ago. He sent me a message mentioning that he noticed my name on the line-up for the festival. We had a brief 'hello' via Instagram message, and I left it there. The next week, I was in Sydney for less than one day and boom! I spontaneously ran into him at a cafe. We had a chat, and I told him that if he was ever in the Byron Bay area to shoot me a message and we could catch up. Well, 4 days later, he was on my doorstep in Byron Bay.

The next few weeks were a haze. I was teaching workshops, swimming in the sea and at the beginning of what I believed was a love story. The next thing I knew, I said 'yes' to moving across the world with this boy – first to London, then to New York. I packed up my whole life within 24 hours.

Yes, it sounds crazy. It was CRAZY! All of a sudden, I was in London on Christmas Eve with his extended family, far from home but following my intuition. The impromptu, radical nature of this life change didn't cause me much fear. I had deep trust that I was there because of the flyer. It was a magnificent mess of an adventure. But, before you get excited, I'm sorry to tell you that he wasn't Prince Charming. It didn't work out.

London was cold and dark – when they tell you the sun doesn't come out for months, they mean it. I left London in a puddle of tears and confusion. I wanted to run straight home but the flyer kept popping into my mind. I truly believed that it was guiding me to something life-changing. However, after a few weeks of travelling, I decided it was time to go home and I flew back to Australia. This decision didn't come easily. I had to surrender and let go of all my expectations. I changed my perspective to look for the positive in my situation. There is power in having the strength to change your mind. My heart told me to let go of my seeking and to release my mind's perception that the flyer was leading me to something magnificent. Maybe I had been wrong?

A week after I got home, I got the call with the green light to write this book. It hit me hard: *The book was the message from the flyer!*

This experience showed me that sometimes you have to go through the dark to get to the light. Sometimes, there is a little heartbreak along the way. There are times when it may take a while to find the positives of a situation, but there will always be positive outcomes, one way or another, which might come in the form of important lessons, and an opportunity to learn and grow.

The more I can learn about myself and the way I navigate the world, the closer I can get to my heart and who I am. Connecting to my heart, and understanding what it wants, enables me to make better decisions in life, and these decisions and choices align me with the life I want to live.

If I hadn't followed the rainbow, I wouldn't have gone to the festival, made the call about my book, met the boy, travelled across the world and learned so much about myself, which would inspire me to share it all with you. I'm grateful for the courage I have to chase the rainbow.

ADHD (AND ME)

Living with ADHD has been a very colourful and interesting journey. It wasn't until my mid-twenties that I finally had an inclination to learn about my differences. Writing this book was a huge challenge. I don't think I sat in a chair once (hyperactivity) … it was written in about 300 different random locations, thanks to my campervan 'office'. Sitting for 20 minutes is hard for me, unless I'm hyperfocused, so I had to keep moving.

Fact: A World Health Organization mental health study from 2016 revealed that an estimated 2.8 per cent of adults worldwide have ADHD. You may be wondering what ADHD is and what it's like to have it. I'll give you a brief rundown of my personal experience.

ADHD is a neurodevelopmental disorder that impacts parts of the brain. It's not a mood disorder like depression or bipolar. The brains of people living with ADHD just work a little differently. The causes of it aren't exactly known, but studies show that genetics play a big role. What's pretty cool is that neuroscience and brain imaging can actually pick up the differences in the brain of someone with ADHD.

I am thankful for my uniqueness. ADHD is not a problem, but a collection of traits that results in an alternative way of being. The way my brain works brings challenges like hyperactivity, distractibility, difficulty slowing down or concentrating, and a tendency to overthink things (it's like having a race car as a brain). However, I find it beneficial to highlight the epic strengths ADHD gives me, such as stacks of energy, an abundance of creative ideas and the ability to hyper-focus on tasks. ADHD offers me different ways of thinking and gives me the strength to take leaps, such as to write this book.

I am thankful for my uniqueness

About
This Book

The most powerful question you can ask yourself is *why*? My *why* is the motivation for my lifestyle and healthy habits. If you have picked up this book, it means that you're open to asking yourself that same question. Throughout this book I will encourage you to ask many questions. The more you understand yourself, your dreams and your desires, the more equipped and empowered you will be to take positive actions each day that align with your future.

I identify as she/her and like to call myself a 'warrior woman'. My definition of a warrior is having strength. Strength can mean something different to many of us but, to me, it means a person who knows they are worthy of living the life they crave. It's about having belief in yourself, having your own back in times of need and being able to show up and courageously face all of life's challenges. It's about having respect and love, even when things get messy, and picking yourself up again. It's about being dedicated to your health and happiness and holding value in supporting and caring for others. However, being strong doesn't mean you have to go it alone. We all need supportive people and guidance along the way. That's why I've written this book so, even if we're not together physically, this book is here to support you growing (at any stage of life) in a fast world. It's a safe space that provides you with knowledge, lifestyle practices, wisdom and love.

ASK YOURSELF *WHY?*

Why do you want to take this journey? Because it's YOUR EPIC LIFE and you deserve to experience it with health, love and happiness.

I get it. I know how hard some moments of this magical life can be. I've broken down, lost myself, cried a thousand tears and felt sadness so deep I have left my body. I've experienced chronic pain and mental-health issues. I believe that we are all connected, and so many of us have experienced similar challenges at one time or another. When I realised that the way I was living wasn't sustainable, I knew I had to develop lifestyle habits that would assist me in the long term. The ways of living and thinking I share in this book are now my lifestyle. Without them, I wouldn't be the woman I am today.

I was inspired to write this book because I hope that by giving you a peep into my world and showing you how I stay committed to my health and wellness, it might help you on your own journey. I want to share with you the exercises and ways of thinking – the 'tools' – I have used to clear my own mind, upgrade my lifestyle, heal old wounds, care for my soul, cherish my body and become a better friend to myself.

～～～

My mission is to help others,
See in rainbow colours.

～～～

HEALTHY HABITS, TRUTH BOMBS AND EXERCISES

In this book, you will come across 'healthy habits' – in the context of this book, 'healthy' relates to the body as a whole, including the mind, and 'living a healthy life' means working on different aspects of ourselves and our lives that contribute to our overall mental, emotional and physical wellbeing.

Habits are the things we do regularly and the choices we make each day that become our life. The more positive, health-enhancing habits we add to our lifestyle, the greater effect these have on shaping our lives.

You may see that I refer to some of these as 'key healthy habits'. These five things – journalling, meditation, dance, breathwork and earthing – are the foundation of my lifestyle, my non-negotiable lifestyle practices. I don't necessarily use them all at once, but I've found what works for me. For example, I may use all my key healthy habits some weeks whereas, other weeks, I might dance every day and just do a little breathwork. But the beauty of individuality means you can take my words, ideas and love to create a healthy lifestyle that works for you – a routine that nourishes your mind, body and soul. Add your unique quirk and vibe. The things I share in this book are my personal reflections and may not be suitable for everyone. The suggestions I put forward are all simply meant as ideas for your exploration.

Throughout the book you may notice that I also drop some 'truth bombs' from time to time. These little nuggets of wisdom are things that I wish I had known earlier. You'll also see practical 'try this' exercises, which are designed to further help you on your journey of self-reflection. And again and again it all comes back to asking yourself questions, asking yourself *why?*

I often think to myself, *If only there was a book that could have taught me what I know now.* That's why I'm here. This is the book I would have loved to read. I really hope the healthy habits help you as much as they have helped me. I know what it feels like to crumble, and I know what it's like to experience happiness and love that expands beyond our beliefs.

ATTENTION: ALL GOOD THINGS TAKE TIME

I hope this book helps you to remove any obstacles clouding your vitality, glow and love of life. I am here to help you see and feel your power. To provide you with uncomplicated and practical content that helps you to kick ass. Enter this process with an open heart and mind. Please be gentle towards yourself, take baby steps and stay with it. Go at your own pace. Take your time absorbing these new ways of thinking, because you are about to devour some epic information. If some of this content is confronting or creates discomfort or distress, take some time out to sit with it and reflect. You can also talk about these things with a support network like family, friends or a mental-health professional. Healing takes time, and you never have to do it alone.

The Why is not a quick fix. It's a practical guide that aims to help in the long term. All I want is for you to show up as best you can at every moment. The core of my teachings centre around the following.

- **Authenticity** – Authenticity is about being real, true to yourself and your beliefs and intuition, and not being influenced by others. It's when you feel comfortable living and expressing yourself honestly, and not worrying about how others perceive you.
- **Love** – Love is the core, the centre, of all that heals. It's about working towards loving yourself, loving all beings and loving the earth.
- **Growth** – This is about finding an opportunity to grow despite everything that troubles and challenges you.

In this book you'll learn that it's the small decisions, actions and habits that help create your future. You don't have to wait for your epic life to begin; you can take the first small step to start to live it today.

Some people notice that the benefits come instantly but, for others, it takes time. It's not a race. When I first committed to my health and happiness, it took a while to notice the big changes, and I'm only just noticing some now, years on. But, every step you take will not go to waste.

Stay committed and trust that your work will pay off. Don't worry, as I'll help you with tips on staying motivated. We'll work on using your inner strength to create a deep commitment to creating the life you want. The value of the work is about improvement, not perfection – showing up each day and planting seeds of growth, as well as having patience, love and consideration for yourself.

No matter where you are on your health journey, the past was essential for your growth. It doesn't matter what you haven't been doing. What matters is what you're about to start doing. It's important to realise that everything you have been through was necessary for you to be here with me today.

In this book I share a lot of my story, but it's not just about me. I want to show you how love, health and wellness can nourish you on a beautiful journey of self-discovery. By sharing, we learn that we are not alone and that we are not so different after all. We realise that we are all human and a part of something greater. I encourage you to dance with me through these chapters. I want you to know that I see you and I've got you.

From this moment, you get to make a choice. You get to make a promise to yourself that, no matter what life throws at you, you will pick yourself up and move forward with love, compassion and courage. Now, let's get into it. WHY? Because it's your epic life, you can choose how to live it and you can start today. Are you ready to chase the rainbow? Okay, let's do this!

Part 1
CLEAR YOUR MIND

Thinking Big
and Small

I practise the philosophy of 'thinking big and small'. I was inspired to develop this method of thinking in the early stages of COVID-19. When the devastating news and impact of the pandemic hit, I found myself feeling uneasy. I'm sure many of you have experienced, or are still experiencing, hardships as a result of the pandemic too.

My feelings of uncertainty made me explore ways of thinking that would allow me to stay present, but still allow me to expand my mindset with big thoughts. I asked myself, *How can I think about the future but not try to plan my next few months or years?* So, I focused on thinking big and thinking small. Practising these two ways of thinking can serve us well and support us in life.

Thinking big is necessary for growth and transformation, as it inspires us to look forward and work out the qualities and goals we crave for our future. Without defining where we want to go, we cannot work each day to become better. *Think big* when it comes to long-term growth. You might ask yourself questions such as: *Where do I want to go in my life? Who do I want to be? What is the large goal?* We have to think big to gain clarity on our goals of growth. Thinking big helps us strive to become a better person, lover and friend.

On the other hand, we need to *think small* to remain present, in the now. Thinking small is about appreciating what is right in front of us on a daily basis. We also need to focus on the small things we can do today, which will help us in the long term to benefit the BIG PICTURE. Fixating only on the big and getting stuck in thoughts of the future or the past can remove us from the magnificence of the *right now*, such as seeing the dreamy colours of the sunrise on a morning walk or feeling the ocean breeze on our skin.

The key is to integrate these two ways of thinking into our daily lives to remain present and yet to realise our longer-term goals. This can be likened to the Eastern principles of Yin and Yang. According to Taoism, Yin and Yang are said to represent dualism, polarity and balance and show how two halves or opposites (light and dark, calm and chaos) achieve wholeness and equilibrium, which is how thinking big and small can be viewed.

There are definitely things in life we can't control, but there are just as many things we *can* control. These include our values, the way that we treat ourselves and others, our actions and our lifestyle habits. These are all choices. It's what we do and how we think on a daily basis that shapes us. Change and breakthrough are an accumulation of all the little moments. These moments can be as simple as showing respect to someone we meet or speaking to ourselves with loving kindness. Every day is an opportunity – our opportunity.

WHY IT'S GOOD TO ASK QUESTIONS

I was feeling flat. My world had taken a tumble. I was freshly single after the end of a long-term relationship and on a quest of rediscovery. My motivation had melted down the proverbial drain. I had forgotten my purpose. I had lost touch with my dreams and desires. I realised that not having clarity about my dreams (aka the life and future I desired) had stopped me from moving towards becoming the person I wanted to be.

I purchased some new books. One was an audiobook on high performance in relation to exercise. My interest in sport had me seeking new methods to improve my training. I was a few months into training for a half marathon and, 10 kilometres into a Sunday morning run, the audiobook in my ears struck me with one of those lightning-bolt moments of clarity. *OMG*, I thought. It was like the clouds had parted, and I realised what was missing: I had failed to see the goddamn big picture! I had been searching for meaning, but taking turn after turn with no destination. I had forgotten to ask questions. I had forgotten to ask *why?* No wonder I was feeling flat.

I asked myself the questions below, and now might be a great time for you to do the same. So, grab a pen and paper (or use the Notes section of your phone) and ask yourself:

- what kind of person do I want to be in 5 or 10 years?
- what do I want my life to look like?
- what do I want my friends and family to say about me?
- what attributes and qualities will I have?

I spent a few days asking myself these *big* questions. Once I uncovered my answers through journalling, I was finally able to put together the pieces that I had been missing. I defined my dream destination. I understood *why* I needed to change my actions. Diving into my mindset by asking myself questions, and asking *why*, enabled me to see what I needed to do to become the woman I desired to be in 5 or 10 years. I saw my future by thinking *big*. From that day, my internal and external world transformed. Then I used 'thinking small' to figure out what my daily mindset needed to be and what habits and practices I could implement to stay present but still be driven by my **BIG** goals. My life took a positive turn, and I was finally back on track to living the life I desired – an **EPIC** life.

Journalling and Mapping

J ournalling is a safe space for healing and dreaming, and it can help us to understand and learn about ourselves. Journalling as a health practice can help us to express our feelings, struggles, thoughts and desires. My pen-to-paper practice provides me with a tool to forgive, surrender and release what's no longer serving me.

Journalling is a non-judgemental space just for you. No one needs to see what you write. You can make it beautiful with colours and collages or scribble things into your journal and then later rip them out. This practice is like any in the sense that, the more you do it, the greater the impact and the more beneficial it will be. Try and dedicate time to write daily or weekly.

It's easy to suppress our thoughts and feelings. Often, we are not aware of how we really think and feel until we spend time checking in with ourselves. Journalling creates the space for us to tune in with ourselves before the boat gets rocked or the shit hits the fan.

JOURNALLING

Here are some simple ways to start journalling.

- Mapping out your goals, dreams and values.
- Writing down your top daily and/or weekly tasks.
- Making a nourishment list (things that fill you up).
- Recording your repeated thoughts.
- Writing down daily affirmations.
- Having a go at creative storywriting.
- Letting out all your feelings.
- Making a list of new things to try.
- Setting a daily intention of how you want to 'feel' and list actions to create this feeling. (For example, I want to feel 'creative', so I will try some art and dance.)

Mapping Your Goals, Dreams and Values

I use my journal to map out my core values, dreams and goals. Whenever I'm feeling a little stuck or at a plateau, I come back to this practice. Writing down what is important to me and what I want to achieve helps me to realign. Through reflection, I can figure out what I need to do to create the best version of my future.

Here is an example of a values list.

- Spirituality
- Balance
- Authenticity
- Responsibility
- Compassion
- Courage
- Trust
- Integrity

>>

Weekly Planning

Personally, I don't do well carrying around a regular 'diary'. I like to use my journal to map out my week so I can create a list of things I can do to fill my cup. This helps me to make sure I'm carving out enough time for play and not just work. I have the firm belief that to be happy, healthy and give to others, we need to take care of ourselves first. It's extremely important to make sure you are taking time out each week to do things that make you feel good.

Create three simple lists.

1. Record your non-negotiable commitments, meetings or work schedule.
2. Create a to-do list of the things you want to get done for the week. I like to highlight the five most critical.
3. Create a list of things you would like to do just for you. These are things you enjoy and that make you happy. For example, yoga classes, daily workouts, a massage or a breakfast date with a friend.

Daily Thoughts and Feelings Record

A simple tool for getting swirling thoughts or ideas out of your head is what I like to call 'writing it out'. It's very healing to write down your scrambled thoughts and feelings onto paper. These can be things that are bothering you or things that are making you happy. It's your choice!

If your 'daily record' is something you wish to release that is not serving you, try the following.

1. Write the thought/s down in your journal.
2. Pause.
3. Take three deep breaths and, on your final exhale, release everything you don't need. Let the journal hold it for you, so your mind is clear.

Intention Setting

Daily: Spend a few minutes in the morning setting your daily agenda. Choose an intangible word that you want to base your day around.

For example:

- 'Today I'm going to feel ...' 'happy', 'calm' or 'inspired'.
- Choose three simple things you will do to get yourself there, such as 'meditate', 'read an inspiring book' or 'eat mindfully'.

Weekly: Set weekly intentions in your journal. Try to keep it simple with one or two things. It's best to start small and then set bigger intentions when you feel more comfortable.

For example:

- 'This week I'm going to ...' 'move my body every day' or 'spend time in nature'.

Your journalling is unique to you. If you want a journal that contains only illustrations and no words, then that's rad too. There are no rules. Listen to your heart and experiment until you find ways of expressing yourself that feel natural to you. All that matters is that you are putting pen to paper. Your journal is a safe space for you, and no one else.

Mindset

Your mind creates your reality. The mind is the powerhouse, so to thrive we need to implement practices to clear and expand the mind. In this chapter I will introduce some methods to elevate your consciousness so you can become more aware of your mindset – your way of thinking – and its effect on your life.

But first, let me tell you something. It doesn't matter where you have been or what your past looks like. What matters is where you are going. You have the power to create and manifest the life you desire. You are a warrior, and it's time to start driving down the road of the life you truly deserve. Is today the day you give yourself permission to become the person you have always dreamed of being? You can start right now, in this very moment, by using your imagination. What you think, you become.

Positive psychology is an approach that explores how we can cultivate qualities such as resilience, joy and meaning in life, rather than trying to 'fix' or diminish things that trouble us. The science of this positive way of thinking led to the development of cognitive therapy in 1967 by Aaron Beck. Martin Seligman, a student of Beck, then went on to pioneer what is known today as 'positive psychology'. Practising methods of positive psychology help to support you in navigating life's changing, and sometimes turbulent, waters.

Psychologist and author of *Mindset*, Carol Dweck, studies human motivation and mindset. Her work teaches about two mindsets: fixed and growth.

- In a fixed mindset, people dread failure and believe their basic abilities are fixed traits. They tend to avoid feedback and trying new things. This mindset can be seen in thoughts or beliefs like: 'I can't get better', 'I can't start something new' or 'I fail at everything'.
- Individuals with a growth mindset understand that learning comes from failure and that their abilities and skills can be developed and improved through effort and trying new things. They often welcome criticism as a means to improve, and to learn from their failures. The thoughts in this mindset are more like: 'I can get better', 'I can learn new skills' or 'I learn from my mistakes'.

Dweck's research shows how our conscious and unconscious thoughts affect our health and our lives, and how changing and becoming more aware of our mindset and internal dialogue can impact our ability to improve. This is how positive psychology has enhanced my world and my quality of life – helping me to uncover habitual patterns and limited thinking.

The way we think is influenced by many factors, such as our upbringing, childhood environment, life experiences, personality and relationships. Our thoughts shape our reality and affect our world. Change our thoughts and perceptions, and we can *change our world*. When our thoughts are negative, our perception of the outside world will also be shadowed. The thoughts we have influence our emotions, and our emotions influence our actions. If we wish to take more beneficial actions, we should prioritise and practise improving the health of the mind.

If you are dedicated to the work of creating a more positive mindset, chances are you will experience an epic upgrade to your life and less internal suffering from everyday life events. No matter where you are or where your mindset sits, you can begin to rewire the thoughts of your mind to create a more positive and loving internal environment. In this book we will explore some methods I have found useful.

OVERCOMING ANXIETY

As a young girl, I was always so confident and sure of myself. But, as time went on, my life changed drastically. I was living alone and working in film and TV in both Australia and the US. The pressure of the industry, and the pressure I put on myself, began to affect my mental health and for a few years I had an intimate dance with anxiety.

I would dream of doing the things I do today, but never imagined I could. No matter where I went, my anxiety followed. For years I tried to run from it, but you can't escape from yourself. No matter how far and wide you travel, until you find peace and a home within your heart, nothing will change.

Anxiety is often most prevalent when we are thinking and living in the future – feeling stressed and worried about what's to come. As I evolved and developed an understanding of my anxiety, I realised I was not just longing for places to travel and things to see, I simply wanted to escape my own head.

The road to finding a home in your heart is rewarding. But it doesn't happen overnight. It takes time. However, if you work on building fortitude and practise more self-love and compassion, one day you will realise how far you've come. My transformation unfolded slowly. It started with acceptance. I stopped ignoring the way I felt and began to seek to understand this part of me. Journalling, meditation, mindfulness, self-reflection and asking questions all helped. I noticed that the more I accepted my feelings, the more space I had to transform them. I stopped running away from myself and started embracing this important part of me. I looked at my anxiety as a place I could grow from. The power of mindfulness – which I explore in the next chapter – will support you on this journey.

HARD DAYS ARE OKAY

Before we go on, I should tell you … it's okay to have bad days. It's okay to cry. We don't have to pretend that everything is great when it simply isn't. I like to see the moments when I cry as an emotional cleansing. I welcome them with open arms. Everything we *feel* is valid – it's the *thoughts* in the mind that may not be true. Emotions are a gift and it's important to feel all our feels.

There are days when everything can feel easy. Then there are days when things can feel downright shit. At these times I find it useful to try not to view my days as separate and remind myself that the polarity of our emotions and days can create balance and equilibrium – the Yin and Yang. The days of happiness and the moments of sadness. The up and down, ever-changing flow.

Emotions will come and go. There is no bad or good emotion – each feeling is valid and can act as a teacher. Struggle often comes from resisting or trying to control and suppress what we feel. Things become easier when we lean into feelings, rather than backing away from them. The sooner emotions are felt, the sooner they can dissolve. On the difficult days, I remind myself of the famous adage, 'this too shall pass'. The more I embrace my emotions and let them flow through without judgement, the more peaceful things become.

Some days, you may feel emptiness or sadness for no apparent reason. Maybe it's from loneliness or stress from a past incident, or perhaps there is nothing wrong at all, but there's no need to label or judge your feelings. When you are experiencing challenging emotions, I encourage you not to distract yourself with things such as social media or surfing the web. Sit in your body and let yourself explore what arises, without judgement. Breathe. Can you use what's arising as an opportunity to remove things you don't need to hold on to anymore?

Living a mindful, authentic life means showing up for yourself through all shades of emotions. It's about choosing to take responsibility and cultivate loving kindness for everything you feel. Be honest with how you're feeling. Honesty will set you free, creating growth as well as helping you to gain strength.

It's not possible to always be happy and smiling. But, it is possible to try our best to love and embrace ourselves through all the highs and lows. Remember, the sun is still shining and we have nature with us to help keep things in perspective – to clear our minds and reconnect us with our natural spirit. If you're struggling with the down days, I'm here to remind you that you are not alone.

Mindfulness

Mindfulness is a technique you can use every day, and it can benefit you in many ways. Put simply, it's the practice of being aware and present in the moment. You can be mindful of your thoughts, and you can practise mindfulness by being present in your daily actions. Mindfulness is also practised by consciously breathing, which can help bring you back to the present. You can harness its power every day, anywhere. I like to view it as a way of meditating while going about daily activities. Once you learn it, it's not something that needs to be forced. It's a way of being that feels natural and soothing.

Without mindfulness and awareness of what is going on, thoughts can go to a 'default-like' reaction or setting. When we experience hiccups and challenges in life, our suffering often sparks from the unconscious default thought patterns in the mind. Without mindfulness, when something challenging happens, the brain may automatically navigate to the negative of the situation. Next thing we know, we are in a negative thought pattern that affects our emotions. Our emotions then dictate our actions and decisions, and things start unravelling!

However, through the simple act of mindfulness, you can create space in your inner world to think and react more consciously – in ways that will uplift your life, not limit it. It doesn't take much time to notice the benefits when you practise mindfulness regularly.

HOW TO PRACTISE MINDFULNESS

When your mind begins to fixate on a futile thought, gently bring your awareness back to your five senses.

- What can you see?
- What can you smell?
- What can you hear?
- What can you taste?
- What can you touch/feel?

Keep reminding yourself to slow down and be present. Whenever it wanders, gently bring the mind back to the present moment. I like to practise mindfulness in three different ways – presence in self, presence with another, and presence in the world.

PRESENCE IN SELF

Presence in self represents being fully absorbed in the moment. To be mindful while doing a task is to be truly present in the experience. For example, when you are cooking, instead of stressing about tomorrow or going over yesterday's events, try to experience the moment: smell the ingredients, feel the warmth of the pot on your skin. Think about engaging your senses in the act and find the joy in whatever you are doing.

PRESENCE WITH ANOTHER

Practising mindfulness while around other people means actively listening to what they are saying. Try to experience being with them – what does it feel like? Think about the other person and how they may feel, and how you might be affecting them.

When I reflect on the most memorable moments in my life that I've shared with others, I realise I was harnessing the power of mindfulness – I was genuinely present and absorbed by their company. Failing to practise mindfulness when you're with your loved ones is like losing the magic. Remember that the shared moment will never come again. Can you let the experience of being in their company vibrate through you? Can you be right there with them in that moment?

PRESENCE IN THE WORLD

Mindfulness will nourish you on so many levels. It will allow you not only to witness a sunset, but also to see and feel its beauty. Being truly present enables you to take in the whole experience. You feel more relaxed, fulfilled and open to experiencing all that it has to offer. The present moment reminds us that time is the most precious thing we have. The mind loves to look forward and fixate on things in the future. But if we continually focus our awareness on something outside of where we are right now, we miss out on the power, healing and nourishment of everything that surrounds us *here* and *now*. The present moment is seeking to nourish your mind, body and soul and to positively affect your life.

Notice the tall, beautiful trees on your morning coffee run or share a smile on the street with a stranger. All these moments create little ripples of positive vibration. Mindfulness enables us to experience inspiration, love and connection in any moment.

PRACTISE MINDFULNESS EVERY DAY

We can embrace mindfulness in every activity we do. Practising mindfulness allows us to recognise our habitual ways of thinking. We can use its power to look internally and gain insight into thought patterns that are limiting us. This practice allows us the space to guide habitual ways of thinking into a more positive light.

Humans have a remarkable ability to pause before reacting. Building awareness can help us to pause in this moment, and choose how we want to respond or be affected. Before you approach someone about a conflict, practise mindfulness by contemplating how they may feel or be affected by what you might say. Can you be compassionate and kind with your words? This awareness can allow you to be more thoughtful in the way you respond to life's events.

The practice of mindfulness is simple. Even just 20 minutes of mindfulness each day can help you to feel the joy of the present moment. As you begin practising, it's a good idea to set reminders to 'be mindful'. For example, write on some Post-it notes to stick around your home, or add a 'be mindful' note in your calendar. I make it a priority to walk without my phone a few times a week, with each step acting as a reminder to remain present. I take in the environment and textures that surround me. Mindfulness and presence allow you to live in a way that feels authentic, wholesome and true to you.

Mindfulness is something to be practised, and it's not guaranteed to work first time. There may be resistance as it's something new for your mind to get used to. Don't stress about it. Just relax and breathe and you'll get there!

THE FLOWER

1. Find a flower and hold it in your hand. It can be any size, shape or colour – or find a photo, or simply imagine you are holding a flower.

2. Set a timer for 5 minutes. Sit or stand in stillness, looking at, or imagining, the flower. Bring all of your attention and focus to it. What does it look like? How does it smell? What does its energy feel like? What textures does it have? Take in every little part of it.

3. Every time a thought pops into your mind that is not about the flower, gently guide yourself back to your centre of awareness. Keep witnessing or imagining every little detail of the flower.

Continue this mindful practice until the 5 minutes are complete. Take note of how you feel at the end of the exercise. Do you feel calm and relaxed? Are you more absorbed in the present moment?

THE BREATH

The way we breathe can directly influence the way we feel. To make progress with mindset methods, we can learn to breathe in a way that is mindful, smooth and steady. Let me share with you a recent experience where I had to draw on my breath in order to remain centred in a challenging situation.

It was a crisp winter's morning and I was heading out on my road bike. After a few months of not cycling, I was a little nervous to start riding again. I was familiar with the first few kilometres of the ride, then suddenly I was speeding down a hill, coming to a corner at around 60 kilometres an hour. It was a recipe for disaster. Next thing I knew, it was the death wobbles – an uncontrollable shaking-like sensation that happens when a moving vehicle is out of alignment. If you have ever experienced these devils, you know the poo-your-pants fear they invoke. I felt my thin road bike trembling beneath my body. I swallowed my fear and, in that millisecond, I chose to breathe. All my external senses went dim, and I cultivated a laser-like focus on my breath. I concentrated on my inhalation funnelling down my chest and expanding into the depths of my belly. In that moment, I believed my only choice was breath or death. What saved me was my ability to use belly breathing (see opposite) to cultivate a deep sense of internal tranquillity. This practice allowed my nervous system to relax. My tense body became fluid and its water-like nature allowed me to make a decision of how to flow through and out of those terrifying wobbles.

The breath's ability to bring us back to calmness among chaos is remarkable. Sometimes, we can forget just how powerful the simple act of breathing mindfully really is.

During a stress response, we go into a shallow, rapid chest breath. In this fight-or-flight mode, turning straight to a rambling mind can cultivate more unease. Therefore, the most important thing you can do in a stressful situation is return to a calm breathing pattern.

Belly Breathing

Many of us unconsciously chest breathe (also known as thoracic breathing), hold our breath or breathe rapidly. This kind of breathing is not helping us and can make us feel even more stressed. An efficient breath should funnel deep down into the belly, in a steady, calm way, and the stomach (diaphragm) should expand and contract on every inhale and exhale. This is belly, or diaphragmatic, breathing.

The following exercise is great to try when you are having a stressful or busy day.

1. Find a long piece of string or ribbon and tie it snugly around your waist, in line with your belly button.

2. Start breathing in and out. Every time you breathe in and out you should feel the string tighten and loosen. Keep the string on for as long as possible and see if you catch yourself reverting to chest breathing through the day.

If our breaths are short and shallow, or if we hold our breath, we affect our ability to think clearly, which leads to stress. Busting stress through effective breathing techniques offers us an opportunity to connect back to our highest power. Remember this, because we'll come back to the breath a little later on!

Be Aware of Your Thought Patterns

Building a conscious mindset is like taking a peep into your own thoughts. Having awareness of the thoughts that pop up in our mind can enable us to witness the way we think and also notice recurring thought patterns, which might not always be good! Once we have some clarity about our mindset, we can develop strategies to combat the negative patterns and challenge the mind chatter.

MY THREE-STEP METHOD

During a period of healing and working with a psychologist, I began to understand and uncover ways I could use different mindset methods to help transform my thinking. This was when I became extremely interested in the mind and I started reading books on psychology. I also experienced great benefits to my mental health from learning about Buddhism and reading spiritual texts by authors such as Pema Chödrön and Eckhart Tolle.

Here is a simple three-step method I adapted from these teachings to help transform my mindset. We all have a voice inside our heads – you may be aware of it or you may not. However, this voice isn't actually us. We are the conscious being that hears the thoughts, that witnesses the breath move in and out of our body. A crazy concept to understand, I know! By using mindfulness and this simple positive psychology method, you can identify if the voice is causing you stress or pain.

1. **Awareness** – Notice, watch and observe your thoughts without judgement. Begin to look and listen to your internal world. In this practice, we are trying to recognise defective thinking patterns. Can you begin to notice negative or limiting thoughts? These can run around in the mind and affect us by making us feel stressed, anxious and unworthy.

2. **Separation and Alteration** – After witnessing and gaining some insight about your thoughts, try choosing not to give the negative thoughts your energy. You can do this by using mindfulness: watch them with separation, try not to attach to any of the feelings or allow them to impact your world. Separate yourself from the thoughts. Once you've created this space, can you then create a healthy substitute for the faulty or negative thought? For example, the negative thought you identify may be: *I am hopeless, I will never get fit, I have no motivation.* After recognising this negative thought and creating separation by identifying that it's in fact just a *thought* and not your *reality*, you can challenge it with a more compassionate way of thinking. For example: *I sometimes make errors and have setbacks, but everyone does. I am worthy and I will try my best to keep reaching for my goals.*

3. **Positive Actions** – It is beneficial to try to create some positive actions to help challenge unhelpful thoughts. Are there some habits or exercises you can prioritise to support yourself? For example, if you are struggling with low self-worth, your positive action could be to spend some time journalling to create more compassionate thoughts that you can repeat to yourself in times of need.

THOUGHT SEPARATION 101

During the belly breathing exercise (see page 37), you may have noticed that you can witness the breath moving in and out of your physical body. It's your *awareness* that is paying attention to the breath – you are witnessing the breath, but you are not the breath. This is separation – by using the breath and mindfulness, we can practise separating ourselves from our thoughts. Remember, we are not our thoughts – they are actually separate from our reality. Our thoughts often come from our ego (by ego I mean the 'self', not 'self-conceit') or are wrapped up in the construct we have built of ourselves, and we can use our awareness to witness them and thus separate ourselves from them.

VIBE-KILLING THOUGHTS

Vibe-killing thoughts can come in an array of cheeky disguises. Let's try and catch these bad guys! They might look like false ideas of perfectionism. Thoughts such as: *I'm not an artist, so there is no point in painting.* You may find them hiding in 'shoulds', such as: *I should fit into a size 8*, or 'can'ts', such as: *I can't go to that party. I look terrible today.* I gain huge benefit by creating an inventory of these thoughts and writing down the emotions or feelings that arise from them. Putting pen to paper can help you to recognise the limiting patterns in your mind and figure out positive alternatives. I like to create a table by writing down my positive solutions. You can ask yourself questions such as: *How else can I view this perception? Am I jumping to conclusions? Am I considering the whole picture?*

When combating negative thoughts, I find 'The Work of Byron Katie' extremely useful. Katie refers to 'The Work' as a process of self-enquiry used to question negative and unhelpful thoughts. Katie's practice consists of asking four questions.

1. Is it true?
2. Can you absolutely know that it's true?
3. How do you react, what happens, when you believe that thought?
4. Who would you be without that thought?

The next step is using your imagination to create a *turnaround* to the thought. Here are a couple of examples.

Trigger thought: *I am a bad person for eating that.*
Turnaround thought: *I am not a bad person.*

Trigger thought: *I am anxious and out of control.*
Turnaround thought: *I am grounded and in control.*

Then, I like to follow it up with evidence as to *why* and *how* this thought is truer than the other. The backup evidence could be: *If I had listened, I may not have learned a valuable lesson.*

By doing this, the mind becomes a training place, not a perfect space. This work is a practice. I encourage you to cultivate a loving inner voice that is positive and comes from your higher self (I view the higher self as the 'wise self' – an inner guidance separate from the ego and personality). Using empathy and understanding helps to create a more balanced mindset. Try not to attach to negative whirlings of the mind. Instead, let them flow out and practise using your internal power to create a more accepting, loving environment.

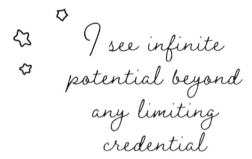

I see infinite potential beyond any limiting credential

ONE STEP AT A TIME

The end goal is to have positive and loving thoughts. However, forced positivity can do more harm than good. You need to meet yourself at your individual stage of growth. If your mind chatter is hurtful and toxic, trying to jump straight to a place that is full of love and joy may not be helpful or even possible for you. If you feel sad or frustrated, suddenly telling yourself you must be happy isn't honouring where you are right now. The most beneficial thing you can do is meet yourself only one step ahead of where you are. I want you to think of this as like climbing a ladder. If you have a toxic thought, your first step on the ladder might just be having an awareness of this thought. Step two might be to cultivate compassion for yourself. Step three may involve exploring a more positive thought. Step four may be having a loving internal dialogue.

Be dedicated to your mindful habits. The more you practise being positive, the more positivity will ripple into your life. Approach rewiring your thoughts like starting a new skill – be patient and trust that your hard work will pay off.

When I first started this conscious thinking practice, I had to be committed and stay focused. At the beginning of my journey, my negative thoughts were consuming my mind. Years on, now my positive perceptions have shaped my world. Most of the time, when a negative thought appears, I can listen to the thought and separate myself from it by using mindfulness and my three-step method. Letting it flow out of my mind, I then try my best to highlight something positive about my circumstance that can benefit my mental health.

DETACH YOURSELF FROM NEGATIVE THOUGHTS

It's okay to have negative thoughts. The work is about understanding that you don't have to grasp onto all these thoughts – this can cause us unneeded stress. You can practise witnessing them and letting them go. I encourage you to begin to watch the mind – let it ramble and think – but separate yourself from its chatter.

As we begin detoxing the mind of unhelpful thoughts, it can also be useful to start looking at parts of our lives that trigger negativity. Are there particular environments that make you judge, compare or talk down to yourself?

There may be particular people that trigger feelings of unworthiness in you. Reflect and evaluate if this is the case. You may like to limit contact with, or avoid, people, places and spaces that don't support you in creating a mindset of success. Pour more energy into things that positively influence you – this could be yoga classes, dinners with caring friends or walks in nature.

'You are not your thoughts;
you are aware of your thoughts.
You are not your emotions;
you feel your emotions.'

– Michael A. Singer, *The Untethered Soul*

POSITIVE SELF-TALK

I encourage you to practise positive self-talk. People flow in and out of your life, but the most important relationship you will have is the one you build with yourself. It's beneficial to grow a positive relationship with your own mind and body. Think about having your own back by showing up and speaking to yourself with kindness, compassion, understanding and empathy.

Life is not always easy. We are such beautifully complex beings, varying from light to dark in different moments. Our human intelligence and capability to experience so much joy means we also have the capacity to experience heartbreak, pain and uncomfortable emotions. Luckily, there are ways you can nourish connection with yourself. Maybe it's a good idea to set the intention to become a friend to yourself through difficult times. Make the decision that you will not tolerate negative self-talk in your mind. Say **NO** to the BS that tries to bring you down.

Speak to yourself like you would a dear friend. Nurture yourself with positive or accepting affirmations, and boost your confidence by telling yourself how well you are doing. Remind yourself of the reasons *why* it is important to build a loving internal environment. For you, these may be to reach your goals and to live a happy and healthy life. You deserve an epic life, and it all starts within.

Replace Negative Self-Talk

If there were only one practice to implement today to improve your life, I would suggest throwing negative self-talk in the trash. You can do this firstly by noticing any negative inner dialogue, and then challenging it by choosing not to believe it. You can even try replacing the negative chatter with something more positive. You don't have to be ready to love yourself yet, but you can create an internal dialogue that is compassionate, understanding and accepting.

YOUR BRAIN CAN BE 'REWIRED'

I walked past the mirror outside my bedroom today and caught a glimpse of myself. I noticed how beautiful I felt and looked, and I unconsciously complimented myself. Catching my reflection in the mirror sparked a flashback. For years, I would look at my reflection and pick myself apart. Today, as I stood there in a mindful moment of noticing my natural state, I had the thought that *I was beautiful* and I was proud of how far I've come in the way I view myself.

In 2018 scientists attempted to map all the neural connections in the brain, basically to work out how the brain is 'wired' and if the connections were stable. However, this study revealed the opposite – that our brain connections are actually dynamic and the brain's neural circuitry can undergo a type of 'rewiring' influenced by factors such as learning, experience and memory formation. As a result, our brains have plasticity, giving us the potential to change the way they work. Adopting a growth mindset is about believing that we can heal, change, improve and grow, and this brain-rewiring evidence is essentially showing us that this is possible on a neural level.

Our brain, thoughts and outlook on life can all be rewired. However, when I first started this work, it was hard. My practice of saying compassionate or positive things about myself often brought discomfort and resistance. But, just like it did for me, my hope is that your hard work will pay off too.

Each time that you choose to spread more love into your world, the closer you will get to making it your reality. What you think, you become. So, let me remind you, you are enough. You are beautiful exactly as you are. You just need to believe it yourself.

About
Meditation

Meditation is a practice that allows me to just *be*. It helps me find contentment and acceptance in exactly where I am and who I am right now. I view meditation as a tool and a place to train for the challenges we face in life. It can change how we relate to ourselves and the way we react to the world around us. I believe meditation can help us practise detaching from our thoughts. If we can witness the thoughts of the mind in meditation, we may begin to further understand that we are not the mind.

The origin of meditation dates back to the Vedas – ancient Indian texts from around 1500 BCE. No one knows for certain how long humans have been practising meditation, but studies by Svend Davanger suggest it may be as old as humanity itself. There are three primary forms of meditation: concentration, contemplation and self-transcending. My first experience with the concentration method was during my 300-hour Jivamukti yoga and meditation training.

Since then, I have discovered a love for the self-transcending method, specifically Vedic meditation, an ancient mantra-based meditation that I learned from qualified teacher Rich Muir.

You may have a good idea of the importance of practising meditation. But the big question is, do you do it? Okay, okay, I know it may initially feel like another thing on your to-do list, but I suggest that you take the time to understand why meditation is important. Yes, it can be challenging to create the initial motivation to meditate (especially if you expect to be enlightened after one session). Maybe you start practising, but stop a few days later. We are all conditioned to want quick results, but when it comes to meditation, we need to understand and respect the journey and the importance of patience.

It's a good idea to think of the reasons why meditation may benefit you. Reminding myself *why* I meditate is what drives my motivation to practise. I meditate because it positively affects my life and helps me to feel more grounded and connected. Some of the benefits I notice are the way it calms my nervous system and thoughts, helps me manage my ADHD, helps me make better decisions and improves my creativity and acting performance. I initially became interested in meditation because I didn't like the way I felt when everything was a little scattered. When I meditate, I feel like I'm bringing my body back into balance, recharging my brain and internal batteries.

'It is only when the correct practice is followed for a long time, without interruptions and with a quality of positive attitude and eagerness, that it can succeed.'

– Patañjali, *The Yoga Sūtras of Patañjali*

Meditation makes me feel like a melting marshmallow

Here's a Q&A with my meditation teacher, Rich Muir, to explain the philosophy behind the practice.

Q: Rich, how would you describe meditation?
A: Meditation is the beautiful practice of redirecting our attention 180 degrees inwards. Many of the best teachers on the planet over the past thousands of years have been dropping clues that what you seek is within. Meditation is the tool and technique to take the journey.

Q: Why do you think we should meditate?
A: We all come to meditation for different reasons. For some, it is to remove the heavy weight of stress, anxiety or depression. For others, it is to be more present with their loved ones or to increase their performance in the work or creative space. For others, it may be a wish to connect with something beyond themselves, call it spirit, God or consciousness. For most of us, the calling comes packaged in its own unique way.

The world is one heck of a stressful yet exciting ride. Did you know that it is suggested we are consuming the same amount of information in a single day than our ancestors did 250 years ago in a whole year? Crazy, right? But think about it. Flashback to what day-to-day life looked like then, then fast forward to today – our nervous systems are under constant bombardment. Even if you don't feel stressed, your nervous system is feeling it ... kinda like if your mobile phone has 15 apps open. It chews through the battery so much faster than if you're running one program at a time.

Q: Can you explain the different methods?
A: There are many styles of meditation. They all fall into the following three primary forms, and they all work differently on

the nervous system. It is like a gym – if you want cardio fitness, you are not going to focus on lifting heavy weights. You have to find the right type for you.

Concentration – This involves concentrating on your breath, a candle or a mantra. This style activates the left hemisphere of the brain (the side for rational thinking and logic). It is good for developing concentration and focus, yet many people find this a challenge, as with minds that are in hyperdrive, it is hard to concentrate during meditation. This can lead to a sense of frustration.

Contemplation – Bringing our awareness to the present moment without judgement, allowing things to come and go and bringing our awareness back to an anchor, i.e., the breath. Mindfulness practices and guided meditation fall into this category. This style activates the right hemisphere of the brain (the side of present-moment awareness and big-picture thinking). There are many apps you can use to try contemplative forms of meditation.

Self-Transcending – Using a mantra and an effortless technique without concentration. This style activates both hemispheres of the brain. Transcendental meditation and Vedic meditation use a mantra, spoken aloud, which is designed to be a nice sound that relaxes the mind and body. It is good for stress and brain coherence, and a powerful way to bring the body into a deep state of rest.

Q: Is it possible to be 'too busy to meditate', or is that a meditation myth?
A: Science shows that we have between 60,000 and 80,000 thoughts a day. A lot of people think their mind is too busy, but

we all have loads of thoughts. We can meditate even with a busy mind. We learn not to judge meditation based on how busy or quiet our mind is. Your mind will think, just like your heart will beat!

Science has shown us that meditation is almost the opposite of sleep. When we sleep, our mind leaves the room, yet the body stays active. When we meditate, the body goes into a deep state of rest, yet the mind is highly aware. Science refers to this as a state of restful alertness.

Therefore, we cannot underestimate the power of this rest and, as a result, meditation has shown to offer a host of benefits, such as:

- reducing the impacts of anxiety and depression
- removing the negative effects of stress
- reducing signs of ageing
- improving your sense of wellbeing
- increased creativity
- increased academic results
- a deeper connection to ourselves and that which is beyond ourselves
- improved mental health
- improved relationships
- the ability to respond, rather than react.

HOW TO BEGIN MEDITATING

Start Small – Start with setting aside 5 minutes to meditate daily, preferably at the same time each day. I wouldn't suggest trying to meditate for 15–30 minutes on your first time, as we are aiming for long-term consistency. Once you have been doing 5 minutes each day for 2 months, then you can increase your duration time by about 5 per cent each week. All good things take time.

Commit – Commit to the practice. Know your reasons why and make a pact with yourself to start to meditate. I have a *Meditate* poster that I stick on my kitchen bench each evening before I go to sleep. When I wake up in the morning and grab a glass of water, I see the poster and I am reminded of my mission. An iPhone reminder is also a great way to help you stay on track during the initial stages.

Practise – Practice does not equal perfect, that's not what it's about. It's about being consistent, showing up and trying to stay present. It's not about being 'good' at meditation. It doesn't matter how many thoughts arise or how many times you hold onto a thought. Keep returning to the centre of your awareness if you get distracted. Don't give up before you notice the epic life benefits.

Key
Healthy
Habit

MEDITATION

Below are three different meditation techniques you may like to try. I have adapted these over the years and love them.

1. Mantra and Affirmation Meditation

Choose a mantra to focus on. You can design your mantra around your personal needs. You may wish to write a sentence on forgiveness or self-love to repeat during your practice. Here are some I like to use.

- *Let go:* On my inhale, I say 'let' in my mind and on my exhale, I say 'go'. I repeat this 'let go' on every breath.
- *I love and accept myself.*
- *I am strong.*

2. Senses Meditation

This meditation focuses on your senses, one by one. I like this practice for easing anxiety because it gives my mind something to focus on. Sit with your eyes closed or open, whichever you prefer. For a few minutes, focus on each different sense.

- What can you hear?
  (Notice all the noises near and far.)
- What can you smell?
- What can you feel?
- What can you taste?

- What can you see? (If your eyes are closed, maybe it's the inside of your eyelids.)

3. Music-Cleansing Meditation

I recommend good-quality overhead earphones for this exercise, but any will work. Lie down somewhere comfortable and put on a song. My favourite artist to listen to during this practice is Bon Iver. All you need to do is relax and listen. Listen to every beat of the music. Let the sounds and rhythm radiate through your physical body. Tune in to the way the music feels and sounds. Let all your thoughts disappear. Let the music dance around your body and vibrate into your cells. Bring all your attention to the sounds and vibrations of the beats. When a thought arises in your mind, return to the experience of the song. I find this meditation especially powerful after a difficult period or when things are tough. It's my favourite technique to use after yoga – especially during a full moon. It helps me shed what I no longer need, and release stress from my mind and body.

Authenticity

Authenticity is the real MVP. Authenticity, to me, means expressing yourself and living in a way that's true to you. It's about being real. It represents feelings of freedom in my life. When I'm expressing myself authentically, I feel more connected to my heart. I believe authenticity is built from deep acceptance and self-love. For me it means constantly tuning in to the way I feel and acting in accordance with my individuality by embracing my unique personality traits, intricacies, likes and dislikes. I view authenticity as a practice that asks me to constantly check in with myself, by asking questions such as: *Does this decision feel in alignment with my heart? Am I doing what others think I should?*

My experiences have shown me that true healing and liberation come when we embrace our individuality. There are many reasons why we can lose touch with our authentic self – they could include self-judgement, worry of what others will think and say, or a fear of change.

Choose to be yourself. I took my first step on this journey by getting to know myself. I started to ask questions such as: *What do I really love? What interests me?* Then, I began to experiment with different ways of expressing and living, taking note along the way of what made me feel good. If you are looking to connect back to your authentic self, you can start today. Experiment by trying activities or hobbies you think you may enjoy, going to events that interest you (even if none of your friends are going) or choosing clothes that express your individual style. Make mood boards – collages of images that can be used for inspiration or as a visual presentation. Can you stop looking outward and begin tuning in?

LIVING AUTHENTICALLY

Learn to trust and embrace your own style and authenticity. If something feels good, back yourself with confidence and positive self-talk. If unhelpful thoughts come up, try to soothe them with the positive psychology tools that we learned earlier (see page 26). Listen to your instincts and gut feelings. What things strike your eye? What colours, outfits, activities or places excite you?

~~~~

I want to be me.
To be free.
For the world to see
Every part of me.

~~~~

To me, living authentically means not saying 'yes' when I really want to say 'no'. It represents honouring the way I feel, speaking my truth and celebrating my interests, hobbies and passions. For example, I love reading studies on health, wearing rainbow-coloured clothing and dancing wildly. The more I embrace these things and share them with others, the more in tune with my authenticity I feel. If you enjoy knitting or reading love poetry, embrace these qualities. Celebrate the things you enjoy, rather than hiding them. If you love going to the library, tell your friends why you like it, as they may want to join you. Others will notice your actions, and it will inspire them to embrace their own differences and uniqueness.

One Saturday evening, I was getting ready to go out with an epic girl gang – some old friends and some new ones. My phone went off with a message from one of my friends that read: *What do you think I should wear?* This moment is an example of the ways anxiety or new experiences can make you doubt yourself. There will always be times when a little voice appears inside your head to make you second-guess

Try this

INDIVIDUALITY

Write a list of all the things that shape who you are and make you original. What qualities and attributes do you have that are unique? When I did this exercise, I wrote: *I embrace all my weirdness. I am a geek and I'm not scared to hide it. Why be ordinary when you can be extraordinary?* I also jotted down: quirky colourful style, random cheek dimple, quick wit, long fingers, enthusiasm.

your decisions, and that's okay! The most important thing is to have awareness of these moments. You can always take a breath, allow yourself to pause, then choose to tune back in with presence. What do *you* want to wear? What ways of dressing make *you* feel good? I know that when I am wearing something that isn't me, I feel off-colour. Wear what makes you feel good. Practise this by trying on different clothing and taking note of what makes you feel your best and at ease in your skin. What are you wearing when you look in the mirror and see a reflection of *you*? Once you start embracing your authenticity, your tribe will resonate with you.

Continually remind yourself of what it means to be authentic. This definition can look different to everyone, but it may involve:

- doing things for yourself
- expressing yourself in your unique way
- being the author of your life and your actions
- having your own opinions that aren't based on other people's
- not seeking approval
- trusting your instincts when it comes to your likes and dislikes.

Judgement and Comparison

Lokah samastah
sukhino bhavantu

– ancient Sanskrit mantra from
The Yoga Sūtras of Patañjali

The mantra above was one I chanted every day during my yoga and meditation training, and translates to: 'May all beings, everywhere, be happy and free, and may the thoughts, words and actions of my own life contribute to that happiness and to that freedom for all'. These words embrace a philosophy of non-judgement and a lifestyle where thoughts and actions are free from toxicity. It also suggests that the way you live your life should contribute to the happiness and freedom of others around you.

I believe we are all one at our core and we all deserve the same respect. Understanding that we are all connected in a positive way can leave you feeling less isolated. Below is a warrior mantra I wrote for my journal.

~~~

I am a warrior woman.
A warrior woman doesn't judge others, she supports them.
She doesn't speak of equality, she is equality.
A warrior woman does not wait for her dreams, she creates them.
She owns her power.
A warrior woman is never lost. She has a home within her heart
and a family among her brothers and sisters.

~~~

RELEASING JUDGEMENT

Failure to recognise that we are all connected can make us more vulnerable to judgement and comparison. If you want to evolve into your highest self, it's important to remove judgement towards yourself as well as towards others.

Releasing this toxicity is not an easy practice, as often wounds or old traumas lie underneath our judgements. We all have them, and if we don't consciously work to move beyond our shadows, we can unconsciously project judgement onto others.

You can release judgement by embracing your story, accepting and sitting in truth with your internal struggle and asking questions to find out if your judgement towards others is coming from a place of discomfort within yourself. Why should we judge others if we don't like to be judged ourselves? Be inquisitive and look into your world. Are you judging yourself or others?

THE LAW OF KARMA

Yoga philosophy teaches about the law of karma. This law states that every action can cause infinite effects. It can help us to understand *why* it's important to live in ways that don't harm. Learning about the law of karma helped me to take responsibility for the way I think, speak and act. I realised that my actions and thoughts don't go unnoticed. If I think negative thoughts about my body, then I start to feel unworthy. If I judge other people for their actions, then I'm creating little ripple-like waves of negativity in my world. I believe that the way we treat others demonstrates the way we feel about ourselves. The more we remove negativity and harm from places we can control, such as our minds or behaviours, the more peace and contentment we can feel. Are there places in your life where you can spread more compassion and kindness? Can you sprinkle love in places of judgement? Can you take a moment to catch thoughts of judgement when they arise, and then choose to think something more compassionate?

Start to plant seeds and create grooves of positive action. Embrace and support people around you. Treat others the way you want to be treated. You can be the change and start a stream of positivity. What you radiate out will often have an effect, attracting more good vibes back to you.

Next time you are out and about and you come across a person with attributes you appreciate, tell them. If you notice someone on the street who is being kind to someone else, then acknowledge it.

Radiate love, compassion and kindness

Don't be shy. Casually connecting with others has boosted my mental health when I've been working in places across the world, away from my family and friends. Bring back the power of positive connection with people around you. Tell them what you like about them. It is time to embrace and support others no matter who they are, how they choose to express themselves or where they are from.

Try this

COMPARISON

Comparison creates unreasonable expectations. Every person in the world is different. It's natural to notice your differences, but comparing the way you look or behave to others can create a cycle of destruction. Here are some exercises that can help you beat the cloud of comparison.

1. Define What Makes You Unique.

Get your journal and write a list of all the things you like about yourself and the features that make you unique. Next to each word, write bullet points on why these characteristics are positive. For example: *I like that I'm extroverted, as it allows me to have the confidence to make friends with strangers. I like my crazy laugh as it makes other people laugh.*

2. Identify Specific Triggers.

If you often struggle with comparison when you are feeling stressed in particular situations, then some guided meditations may be suitable for you. Maybe there is a

>>

particular group of people that trigger you to compare yourself. If so, it could be time to ask yourself if this group is a healthy one for you to spend time with. If you compare yourself to particular people on social media, unfollow them to give you time to work on building your self-worth.

3. Gratitude Journalling.
One of the best ways to combat comparison is with gratitude. Write down the ways you compare yourself to others, and focus on turning the negatives into more neutral or positive outlooks. Here are some examples:

NEGATIVE	POSITIVE
• They are a better dancer than me.	• I am grateful that I can dance.
• They have better style than me.	• I am grateful that I can choose the clothing I wear.

Stay magic!

THE TWO FORMS OF COMPARISON

You may be aware of comparing yourself to others, but did you know that comparison comes in two forms?

COMPARISON OF SELF TO SELF

I often use my awareness to check in with how I'm thinking and feeling. I am hyper-sensitive and very attuned to any mood variations that don't feel right. One particular night I was feeling foggy and disembodied. I realised that mindlessly scrolling through old images on my phone that night had left me in the depths of comparison and unworthiness, with thoughts such as, *I'm not like I used to be.* This false limiting belief was a sign. It reminded me of the power of vowing not to judge and compare myself to a past version of me. Each day you grow and evolve. You are never the same. Therefore, it should seem impossible to compare yourself to who you were in the past. Focus on growth and celebrate your evolution. If we didn't evolve, we wouldn't experience the wonder of the unknown, and life would always be the same and quite boring.

COMPARISON OF SELF TO OTHERS

When judgement and comparison issues arise, we should remember the huge influence that social media can have on our mental and physical health. Scrolling through an Instagram feed can trigger us to compare ourselves to all the people we follow. These thoughts and feelings can begin to leave negative patterns in the mind, bringing down self-love. For many of us, our phones are often the first thing we look at when we wake, and the last thing we look at before bed. It's important to remember that our morning and evening routines are directly influenced by what we consume. I choose not to follow accounts that have a negative influence on my health. I save hashtags on #selflove and #bodypositivity so that I see these positive gems on my phone each day.

It's worth noting that there can be a trickier side to positivity and the wellness space, which can make you feel like you have to completely love yourself or always be happy and smiling. This is not realistic for anyone, no matter how happy and healthy you may be. Make sure to check in with the way you feel. Maintain balance between the real world and the social media world. Take charge and break the cycle by choosing to follow accounts that lift you up.

PS: Did you know that PHONEMO (yup, I invented the word) is a real thing? It's when you get FOMO (fear of missing out) by viewing the social events and lives of others on your phone. Hello, self-inflicted stress! Social media tip: If some of my friends are doing something fun and I can't attend, I make a conscious choice not to watch their Instagram Stories for that period of time. My decision not to subject myself to PHONEMO is a way I help my health rather than hinder it.

Here is a poem I wrote during a phase of my healing. My topic of choice was comparison.

I seek validation from the outside world, but it's just to create noise, the noise to stop me going in. I choose to be with me now to feel all the bubbling under the surface.

Once felt, it can be transformed into the deep love I forgot existed. It's time to release and surrender. You don't need to try to control the uncontrollable. Through embrace, you can shine. The time is now. I have your hand. We will dance together through the ever-changing waters.

Set Intentions Using Creativity

I like to use creativity to set intentions for my personal growth. This may be a good time for you to set your own intention, using a creative form like an illustration, poem or song.

1. Choose an art form. For example, drawing, painting, storytelling or songwriting.

2. Decide on a personal growth theme or something you wish to set an intention for.

3. Get creative – express your feelings through your chosen creative outlet.

Perspective

Most years I travel to Los Angeles for work. On one of these trips, I was up at dawn, waiting for the sunrise so I could wander by the sea at Venice Beach. This beach has a long strip filled with bright lights, sounds and smells. I'm talking buskers dressed in costumes skating on rollerblades, painted dummies, colourful market stalls and dogs dressed in tutus. This is the place you will never fail to see some wacky stuff.

This particular morning, I was feeling a little down and craving that bounce back in my step. The ocean seemed to be calling me. *Oh, why not*, I thought. So, I stripped off and went swimming in the freezing winter ocean. Everyone else thought I was crazy – I got way more looks than the dogs dressed in tutus. But the cold awoke my spirit. I felt clearer and lighter. Wet and dripping, I began walking back to the apartment. As I passed the daily hustle and bustle of the street vendors and their stalls, a pair of glasses caught my eye.

Gold frames and pink hearts – bingo! At that moment, I was inspired. I purchased the glasses with the cash I had for a morning coffee. I put them on, took a deep breath and set my intention. From that moment, I chose to see through love-heart glasses, baby. The frames inspired me. I thought to myself that if I'm wearing love, I will see love.

For the rest of my month in LA, I wore my love-heart glasses, every damn day. On sweaty runs, in supermarkets and on coffee dates, I chose to let the simple intention of these glasses change my perspective and remind me to see and be the love that I needed. And even now when I feel out of sorts, I'll pull out my love-heart glasses and remind myself of the beauty of seeing through love-heart lenses.

THE POWER OF PERSPECTIVE

Perspective empowers me. It shows me that I have a choice in what I highlight, see, think and feel. I can give my attention to the light over the dark and entertain my mind with growth rather than regret. Perspective has taught me to put power at the forefront when faced with fear, and to shine gratitude in places where it may be lacking.

Where attention goes energy flows, which is why limited ways of thinking, or a narrow perspective, can automatically bring our attention to the 'bad' in a situation That's why I say *perspective is a practice*, as it calls for awareness and an understanding that you have a choice in what you focus your energy on.

The simple act of refocusing my perspective has incredibly benefited my mental health during COVID-19. A few months into the pandemic, I realised that instead of focusing on all the ways the virus had negatively impacted my life and all the things I couldn't do, I should instead focus on all the things I *could* do. So I began to reflect on my time during the pandemic, what I had learned, gained, and the positives that arose from having down time. For example, if it wasn't for COVID-19, I never would have got my dog Bee!

Every day and moment is an opportunity. We can choose to see the rainbow through the rain. We can celebrate our wins over our setbacks. Can you begin to see differently and seek places where you can focus on the positive over the negative?

Our daily perspective shapes us, and it dictates our thoughts, actions and reactions. What goes on in the mind influences the person we become in this world. Now you have the opportunity to examine your perspective. Is it helping you or hindering you? The more you focus your attention on the good in your life, the more good you will see, so practise focusing on the positives. What's something good that you can highlight?

- Start to shine more light on your strengths, not your weaknesses.
- Celebrate your wins rather than your mishaps.
- Be grateful for what you have instead of thinking about what you don't have.

Beliefs and Values

'Your beliefs become your thoughts. Your thoughts become your words. Your words become your actions. Your actions become your habits. Your habits become your values. Your values become your destiny.'

– Mahatma Gandhi

Defining what kind of person you want to be and getting clear on your dreams will enable you to uncover the key attributes, beliefs, feelings and values that are associated with becoming the best version of yourself. By 'values' I mean the things that are important to you, which motivate the way you live your life.

If you want things to change, or you are craving to evolve personally, the first step is to get clarity on where you wish to go.

Imagine you are driving a car and taking directions, but you forget to put in a destination ... you will just end up going in circles. This is where I see people struggle time and time again – not being able to make changes, because even though there are good intentions, there is no definable goal.

However, the good news is, you can begin now and create a goal to work towards. You can figure out what you want your future to look like, and define the person you want to become. Once you have this clarity, the work can be done. The body, mind and spirit need to see where the journey leads. Without knowing where you're going, how can you get there?

When my mental health declined and I struggled with an eating disorder, the practice that supported my recovery the most was *asking questions* in my journal. The simple practice of getting a new perspective, and 'thinking forward' to gain clarity on my dreams and goals, changed my life. Here is a snippet of the personal mission statement I wrote at that time, about the person I wanted to become.

Personal Mission Statement

I am a calm and centred woman. I work hard and take care of my mind, body and spirit. I practice meditation to stay grounded. I am brave and I love to meet new people. I welcome every new day and take control of my actions. I treat everyone I cross with love and compassion. I attract kind and respectful people into my life. I radiate authenticity. I am wise and grounded. I am dedicated to helping others. I am a well-established writer and I love expressing my creativity in film and television.

By defining your own personal mission statement and figuring out what you want your life to look and feel like, you will have guidance from your higher self (see Mind Tip on page 126). To achieve the life you crave, the first call of action is defining the essence of who you want to become, which includes your principles and values.

If you are feeling stuck in the mud, fear not, because I have developed a method to break through that mindset! Grab your journal and let's get into it – I bring you the transformational power of 'thinking forward'.

THINKING FORWARD FOR A VALUES-DRIVEN LIFE

You are so much more than the job you do, the amount of money you have in the bank or the material items you own. Let's move beyond these attributes and find out about *you*. To do this, it's time to do some journalling. The questions suggested on the following pages are a guide to get you started. They are similar to ones you have asked yourself in previous chapters, to encourage you to dive into these topics a little bit deeper.

Remember to take your time – there is no rush. If one question in particular jumps out at you, explore it further. Can you add your own questions to get more clarity on the subject? As you work through each question, don't be scared to reach for the stars. If you have a dream or goal, then write it down. There is no such thing as 'too big' here.

If words don't flow with ease, try creating images that capture the essence of your goals. Try methods like mood boarding with Pinterest, creating a poster for your wall or an album of images in your iPhone. Attach feelings, smells and places to your dreams. Use creative influences like playlists of songs that make you connect with your soul. I like to ponder my future self's house. I use my imagination to create my dream environment. I even add in animals, habits, friends and family members. It's a good idea to pin up your vision board, goals and dreams list somewhere you will see it. Having a daily reminder of what matters most to you can fuel your fire, helping you to stay on track.

DEFINING YOUR VALUES

Use the below questions as a starting point, and choose two or three that immediately jump out at you. It's important to start small so that you don't get overwhelmed. It's not about finding the 'right answers', it's about figuring out what you *don't* enjoy and following what you *do*.

Purpose
- What is your mission or purpose in this world?
- What do you care about the most?
- Is there something you want to create or contribute to?
- What are you doing when you forget about the outside world?

As a Person
- Who do you want to become?
- What are the key attributes you want to have?
- What are your strengths and weaknesses?
- What would you like your family and friends to say about you?
- How do you want to be remembered?

Dreams and Goals
- How do you want to feel in life?
- When do you feel happiest?
- What are your goals?
- What are your dreams?
- What do you see yourself doing in 5, 10 and 20 years' time?
- What do you want more of in your life?
- What do you want less of in your life?

Passions
- What do you love to do?
- What are you good at?
- What interests you?
- What do you care deeply about?
- What do you do in your spare time?

DAILY ACTIONS TO REINFORCE YOUR VALUES

Answering these questions will give you a better understanding of what you want. Then you can begin to work backwards to design mini lifestyle hacks to focus on each day. Long-term health and lifestyle changes come from small daily actions. For example, if you want to become a writer and a good cook, your weekly habits could be: writing a creative story three times a week, as well as trying out two new recipes each week. We have to be clear about the essence of *who* we want to become, *why* we are here and *what* our values, beliefs and goals are in order to create the life we aspire to!

HOW DO I KNOW WHEN I'M IN ALIGNMENT WITH MY VALUES?

Your set of values is unique. If a definition of these values doesn't come with ease, then focus on feelings. If your life isn't in balance with your values, you might experience an internal feeling of unease, resistance or aggravation. If you are feeling off, stuck or annoyed, it might be a good time to assess if your lifestyle is in alignment with your values. Look at your daily routine and try to find what parts of it give you nourishment on a mind-body-spirit level. Does your job make you feel fulfilled? If not, then maybe it doesn't align with your beliefs. Do you leave particular social events to return home and turn to something like food or television? It might be an appropriate time to reflect on whether the social engagement was uplifting for you.

Do more of the things that make you feel good and less of the things that don't. Focus on building a core list of activities that fill you up. This fulfilment will begin to ooze into your health and happiness.

OBSTACLES TO YOUR SUCCESS

Nothing comes without work, and there will inevitably be obstacles. These can come in many shapes or forms.

Limiting Beliefs and the 'Shadow Self' – Limiting beliefs and thoughts are the stories that come into our mind that tell us why we can't do something, change or grow. The concept of the 'shadow self' is based on a theory developed by 20th-century psychologist Carl Jung. As he explained, the shadow self is the 'unconscious parts of the personality that our conscious ego doesn't want to identify in itself'. I like to view the 'shadow' as an unconscious part of the ego that is quite negative or on the darker side of our personality. If you catch limiting beliefs appearing as you answer these questions, remind yourself that you are not your thoughts. They are a part of you, but they are not you. Take time to create the space to think about what your true self desires.

Here is an example of a limiting belief I have experienced: *I can't be a writer because I wasn't good at English in school.* I used the following method to overcome this obstacle. Firstly, during a reflection exercise in my diary I recognised that it was a limiting belief. I reminded myself that everyone has the ability to share in their unique way. I found many positive examples of people who became authors and writers later in life. My final step was challenging my old limitations by just starting to write, blog post by blog post, and it all went from there.

Self-Sabotage or Feelings of Unworthiness – If you feel unworthy of reaching for the stars, let me remind you that you are capable of achieving what you want. You are worthy. You just need to trust and believe in yourself. I also experience feelings of unworthiness, and I have to tell these feelings to leave me alone time and time again. If I listened to that distracting monkey mind chatter, I would not be here writing this book for you.

REDEFINE YOURSELF

As you look forward and create the life you want, don't get trapped in an old image. It doesn't matter what you've had or who you were in the past. The whole point of this journey is to grow and expand your consciousness. We hit walls that limit our evolution when we continue to try and be like a past version of ourselves. Looking back on old photos where we perceived our life was 'perfect' or 'happy' is not helpful. It's time to let go of the old. Focus on creating the new, where comparison is less likely to exist.

There is a method to the mindset: It is doing the work by gaining clarity on your values, dreams, purpose and desires. Then, *continually* reminding yourself of your key attributes, dreams and goals. After that, we do something epic.

Redefine yourself and create the life you desire

LET GO AND TRUST

Trust that your reminders will keep you on track. Trust that the *small* actions and habits you decided to do each day will lead you to *BIG* goals. Relax into your journey. If you stay dedicated to your daily choices, then you will be more likely to stay on the path to your dream life.

But what if you change? Don't worry! You can recreate yourself as many times as you like. It's very important to remember that humans are not fixed – we are ever-changing. Flow like water and always stay open and flexible. Defining who we are should never lock us into set rules. Instead, it should enable us to experience a beautiful epic life.

There is no need to get stuck in self-imposed guidelines and regulations. I want you to spend time diving into your inner world, but this process shouldn't cause you stress. If you don't have the answers to the big questions yet, then it's okay. All that matters is that you're asking the questions and expanding your mindset.

Trust your heart

EPIC LIFE EXERCISES

1. Set a daily reminder to label the key attributes of the person you want to become. (You could remind yourself by setting an alarm on your phone or leaving a poster on your fridge.)

2. Find three songs that represent the soundtrack of your epic life. Play those babies and dance around the room. Music helps to create a vibe and it can really engrave the feeling of your life's dreams into your body.

A few times a year I come back to the questions I encouraged you to ask, so I can gain more clarity on my purpose and mission. I set goals and create actions that help me stay on track. Then, I hold onto my values, let go and trust!

I relate this mindset method to acting. Before a show or audition, actors learn pages of script, spend time defining the character and figuring out facts such as their back story, relationships and desires. Once the work is done and the time comes to perform, the only thing to do is *let go*, to trust that the work will guide the scene. The beauty of acting is being truly in the present by listening and responding to the other character.

It is about doing the work and committing to courage. In times of need, we can come back to the work, gain clarity and then, once again, let go.

Setting Goals and Staying Motivated

Are you tired of telling yourself you will do things and then not following through? Are you ready and willing to take the necessary steps to become better at staying motivated? If the answer is 'yes', then read on – you are about to become a master of *goal setting*! Goals should be set in order to achieve success. Motivation will not last unless a foundation, using clearly defined goal-setting principles, is in place.

In the past, you may have set goals but failed to reach them. This might not be due to a lack of motivation, but rather to a lack of knowledge. I've found that there's a structure to setting goals that last. Firstly, we need to make goals realistic, achievable and, as much as possible, enjoyable. Another way to view your goals is by pondering your dreams ... *What excites you? What do you dream of achieving?*

As I learned while I was studying for my personal training qualification, goals require intrinsic and/or extrinsic motivators. *Intrinsic* motivations come from within, are driven by internal rewards and grow from feelings of inner satisfaction, such as wanting to enhance positivity or improve energy because it makes you feel good. Studies show that intrinsic motivations are more likely to last and should be prioritised. *Extrinsic* motivations are related to outside factors, such as doing something because you will receive a reward, for example completing a challenge with the motivation of winning the prize money.

Examples of Intrinsic Motivations:
- Working out because it makes you feel good.
- Eating healthy food because it improves your sleep and energy.
- Taking singing lessons because they make you happy.

Examples of Extrinsic Motivations:
- Eating healthy food with the sole motivation of changing your physical shape.
- Wearing makeup to impress someone else.
- Buying a dress because your friend likes it.

Setting goals doesn't need to be complicated. Here's a simple formula. It's called the SMART principle. You can measure if a goal is achievable by asking, is it:

- Specific?
- Measurable?
- Achievable?
- Rewarding?
- Time-limited?

On the following pages is a practical exercise for creating a motivational poster. Consider the SMART principle as you work through the exercise.

MAKE A GOAL-SETTING POSTER

Take a sheet of paper and a pen and complete the following exercise. If you want to get creative, I suggest making a collage or coloured goal-setting poster for your fridge or bedroom. List the following questions below and write your answers for each. When you have completed the questions, stick them in a place you can refer to when needed. I like to keep my goals in my journal and I send a digital copy to my iPhone for when I am on the go. Referencing them helps me to maintain motivation, reset my intention and connect with my *why*.

1. What Do You Want?

List exactly what you want. Be specific with details such as date, time, location and place. The more specific you can be, the better. Make sure this goal is realistic and achievable in your given time frame. It can be beneficial to start with a long-term goal and then work backwards from there. For example, one of your long-term goals might be to learn three songs on the piano, therefore your short-term goal is to practise three times a week. Another long-term goal may be to have your own health-coaching business, therefore your short-term goal is to save and start a course.

2. Why Do You Want It?

Outline the specific reasons for wanting to reach this goal. The reasons can be physical, mental or emotional. List exactly why. Gain clarity on the positive benefits of making change and the negative impacts for not changing. For example, I want to start to work out 3 days a week because it improves my mindset and sleep.

3. Actions and Habits
What are the actions you need to take and the things you need to do in order to reach your goal? Think about actions and practices you can implement along the journey to reaching the goal.

4. Obstacles
What are the obstacles you may face? Writing them down will help you to prepare for these situations. You can also list some bullet points about what you can do when/if these obstacles come up.

5. Reward
When you reach your goal, what is the outcome? (This is similar to your why, but we are getting specific.) What will you have achieved? To act as an incentive, is there a reward you can give yourself once you are there? This can also be the reward of a feeling like accomplishment. It does not have to be materialistic. I like to work backwards from the main goal and plant little seeds of reward along the journey. This helps to make the process fun and engaging.

6. Visualisation
It's time to visualise! Attach an emotion/feeling and an image to your end goal.

>>

Emotion – Choose an emotion you will feel when you reach the finish line. Write it down and sit with the feeling for a minute or two. Give yourself a taste of what it will feel like. Can you start to embody that emotion *right now*? Visualising the feeling of the end result now will help to turn the goal into a reality.

Image – Find some photographs, or use your imagination and get an image in your head of the end goal. For example, if your goal is to run 10 kilometres, then create a mental image of you crossing the finish line at the end of your run. If your goal is to improve your health, collect some pictures that represent how you want to feel. If you enjoy getting creative, make a mood board or a Pinterest board of your journey, with all the images and feelings attached to this goal.

FIND POSITIVE INFLUENCES

When it comes to goal setting, identifying others who are achieving the goals you dream of is *key*. This isn't about comparing yourself to others, then judging yourself based on what you observe. It's about helping you have confidence in what you want to achieve. Seeing is believing! If you are caught feeling like you can't reach for what you want, seek inspiration from others – either people you know or strangers. What matters is that you let these people inspire you on your personal quest. Find positive people who have created the waves that you desire. Follow them on social media or read their stories. Seek others who have achieved what you wish to achieve. Seeing that it is possible will help to tear down any obstacles in your mind.

KEEP IT GOING

Once all the goal setting is done, you can then implement daily *habits* and *actions* to help you reach the end goal. Remember, it's about continual improvement and commitment, although there may be bumps in the road, which is natural.

Keep your goal list somewhere safe, where you can see it or refer to it easily. When in need, pull it out and reference your *why*. I also recommend getting an accountability partner – tell your family or friends about your goals. Can you ask for support and accountability?

Believe you can, and you're halfway there. Have faith and trust in your power. Fears will always arise, but continuously remind yourself of your true power and follow your heart's desires.

FIND YOUR MOTIVATION

Do you often say that you will do something, but find your motivation quickly seeping down the drain? Maybe you have a list of things you want to do, but keep failing to do them. We have all been there.

Motivation can look different for everyone. It can sprout internally or externally, growing from places such as values, needs, emotions, wants, pleasures and beliefs. My motivation comes from believing in my power. It stems from my craving to grow and improve. It's built from a strong connection to myself. This connection is my internal drive and strength. This is an epic life – one of a warrior.

The more I strengthen my internal world by gaining clarity on what is important to me, and practising mindset methods, journalling, self-reflection and meditation, the more motivation cements itself in me. My goals are important and they are guided by my values.

Knowing my values helps me to make appropriate decisions. I like to refer back to them before I take action. My values are built from listening to my heart. Motivation looks different for everyone. Find out what helps keep the spark in your life.

STAYING MOTIVATED

If you're having difficulty staying motivated – and let's face it, it's probably going to happen at some stage – the following points might help explain what's happening.

Not Knowing WHY – Why is this goal important to you? Why do you want it? For motivation to last, you should know *why* you want to achieve your goals. It could be that you are craving a sense of purpose or you want to become the best version of yourself. My motivation to run and move my body every day comes from knowing how good it makes me feel and the way it positively impacts my life. I am motivated to improve in running to show myself how strong I am and how I can do anything I set my mind to.

Spend time gaining clarity on *why* you want to implement a change or new habit. Can you define the positives and negatives of this behaviour? Remember, it's important to regularly remind yourself of these reasons.

Thinking the Journey Should Be Easy – I'm sorry to tell you, but nothing great comes with ease. Oh, don't we wish it did though! Living an epic life means that you hold yourself accountable for showing up. Understand that there will be days that are challenging and times when you want to quit. In these moments, you can practise self-discipline. For example, you could use the goal-setting principle we went through earlier to create a goal of running a half marathon. You could commit to running a couple of times a week, and then you just gotta show up and do it! You need to cultivate the discipline to lace up your shoes and run each day. Once again, my self-discipline is driven by my *why*. Connecting my goals to my *why* is what gets me out of bed at 6 am and guides me to my yoga mat or to the street for a run. It's a decision I make because I know it positively impacts my day and my life.

A Lack of Self-Love – I see having a lack of motivation as an opportunity for more love. Lack of, or low, motivation can often arise from internal feelings of unworthiness or low self-worth. The simple act of prioritising self-love could be what you need. I know that building self-love isn't always easy. It's a process, so try to be kind and compassionate towards yourself along the way. The stronger the love-filled connection with self, the greater the feelings of worthiness and confidence you will have, and the stronger the desire for growth will be.

Not Having the Correct Goal – If your goal is externally driven or not aligned with your core beliefs, you may hit a wall. Yes, there could be blocks in your road for a good reason! Examples of goals that may be misaligned could be: wanting to lose weight when you are already at a healthy weight range for your body type, or wishing to become good at an activity to impress someone else and not because you want to. These goals may be coming from the ego, external pressure or a mix of both. Ask yourself if it's really what *you* want, or if you are striving for this goal for external gratification or from a lack of self-love or self-worth. I believe the motivations that will last need to come from the internal world. They should align with your purpose, your values and your heart's desires.

Handing Over Your Power – It's easy to sit back and lack motivation if your power is turned over to dismissive thoughts. We all get limiting beliefs and false perceptions that slap us in the face, and they can stop us from reaching our goals before we have even started. I recommend creating an inventory of the patterns in the mind that may be hindering your success. Here are some examples of their disguises.

- You may be interested in improving but get stopped by a thought such as, *I am not …* or *I can't …*

- You see someone doing something you want to do but get stopped by a thought such as, *they can because they are ... or they have ...*
- Other examples include: *I am unworthy, ugly, not good enough, not smart enough ... or I'm not skinny enough. I can never be a painter. I have never been good at dancing, so why should I start?*

What false beliefs are you walking around with that are limiting your potential? Taking note of what they are can help you separate yourself from these thoughts. Once witnessed, you can create the space to challenge them and stop believing them. (See page 39 for more information.) You don't have to let false beliefs and perceptions stop you from living the life you dream of. Try not to let little lies manifest roadblocks in your life.

CREATE A FAB VOCAB

The words you speak or think don't go unnoticed. Words are powerful and, even if they are not said out loud, they can halt your success. Try and remove dismissive words from your vocabulary. Phrases or words that you may be unconsciously saying or thinking may include 'should', 'but', 'hope', 'maybe', 'might', 'I'm not' or 'I can't'.

It is helpful to create a fab vocab because the world that you see is a projection of the way you think. When you can alter the projection of your mind, you can alter the world in which you live. Even the simple practice of saying *no* to any limiting vocabulary can create a change in your mindset. 'No' can also be a good word to use for setting boundaries or declining offers that you don't have the energy to take on. Speaking with confidence and certainty can engrave your desires into your mind. Try and catch your limiting vocabulary when it gets in your way. Instead of saying, *I might try to learn how to paint*, a fabulous substitute could be, *I will have a go at painting*.

You don't have to be good at something to do it. You can run or paint just because you enjoy it. I set a goal to learn to play an instrument recently. I got a ukulele for Christmas and, my gosh, I was terrible for a solid 3 months, but I was okay with it. I *love* playing my uke; I don't care that I am not good at it. You are allowed to do any activity just for joy. Just for you.

READY, SET, GO!

Just as your thoughts influence your actions, your actions can influence your thoughts. Sometimes it just takes a little push at the starting line to create momentum, helping your thoughts to become more positive. If you're feeling stuck, then maybe it's time to stop thinking about it and just start. It could be exactly what you need to gain momentum for your motivation. It's important to remember that motivation gets easier. Its energy grows the more you start to *move* and *do*. Try something small, then let the small manifest into the great.

Remember to reflect and see your path in others. For example, you could seek individuals with inspiring fitness journeys and use them as your motivation. Everyone starts somewhere.

Building your epic life means being brave and believing that you can work towards *anything* you wish for. You are capable of achieving anything you set your mind to. Sometimes it can be as simple as just getting out of your own goddamn way.

It's not the end goal that counts. No matter how hard we work, sometimes we may never reach our end goal. The most important thing is the commitment to have courage, try our best and work for what we desire.

Part 2

LOVE YOUR BODY

Your
Beautiful
Body

I like to think of the body as a divine place where we can experience the beauty of life. Our body never wishes to cause us distress or harm. It is a gift – one that thrives on love, care and pleasure.

I believe that everything in the universe is connected. Our mind, body and soul are related, and we are connected to the animals, plants and the environment. Just like the way toxic chemicals can harm our planet, abusing the body can, in effect, abuse the mind.

Living in a fast-paced world, it's easy to lose touch with practices that keep us in tune with our bodies. Many of us spend hours every day on the phone, watching television or distracting ourselves in other ways. This causes us to 'disembody' (more on this later). But what if we used some of this time to experiment with things that strengthen our connection with, and understanding of, our body? These habits will encourage an easier relationship with our body and may also cause us to feel happier in other areas of our life.

If you are disconnected from your physical form or have forgotten how to *be* your body, I'm excited for you to reconnect and feel the lightness of 'embodiment' (see page 108). If you have a focus on your external image that causes suffering, let's unpeel the layers. It's time to bring back the magic. Shine in the body, shine in the soul.

ASK FOR HELP IF YOU NEED IT

Eating disorders are a serious mental illness. Please, if you are struggling, talk to a support network or seek professional help. See page vi at the beginning of the book for information about where you can find support. Vulnerability and asking for help is a brave act. If these personal stories about body image and eating disorders trigger any negative thoughts, you might like to journal about any confronting or distressing thoughts that may arise.

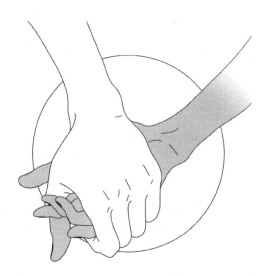

Overcoming My Eating Disorder

I haven't always had a positive relationship with food, eating and body image. During adolescence, I lived in a pretty healthy household. However, any chance I got, I would run to the service station across the road to buy whatever junk food I could afford. I believe my relationship with food served as a coping mechanism. In primary school I was put down for my 'chubby stomach' and I have distinct memories of getting bullied for the way I looked. At that age, I didn't know how to deal with the sadness I felt, so I would binge eat to try to distract myself from, or suppress, my emotions. This would often leave me feeling worse than before.

A new high school provided me with a fresh start. Attending a performing arts school, my creativity soared. I found a love for running and skateboarding. As I dived into acting and started working in the entertainment industry, I was happy and became motivated to begin working on my health; eating better and moving more. I no longer found myself seeking comfort from food. I went vegetarian at 13, then vegan for a few years (this diet wasn't right for me long term). Everything felt quite good until years later, the pressure simmered and once again my relationship with food got rocked.

I met with a modelling agency in Sydney after starring in the TV show *Puberty Blues*. The two agents said I would fit in great with the agency, but my body was 'too big'. They took my measurements and commented on my figure. *You're not good enough, your body is too large,* was my interpretation of their words, which ricocheted through me. My heart felt like it was being stabbed.

Those few simple words caused a hurricane of emotions I didn't know how to deal with, which led me down a difficult path. At the time, I didn't have the perspective, tools and core beliefs that I needed to deal with those challenging emotions.

After that, I found myself in a year-long battle with bulimia. Eventually one of my family members found out and told me I needed to stop. I buried my feelings and forced the behaviour to stop, but my inner work wasn't done. I still had a disconnection – an internal desire for mind-body-soul nourishment – but I pushed it all down and kept living life.

Over the next year, I became intrigued by nutrition. I *loved* learning more about health and the benefits of eating well. Thanks to ADHD and hyper-focus, I was able to absorb a lot of information. I read every book and studied every diet. I learned so many facts about food but still hadn't learned how true health is all-encompassing and is not about finding the perfect diet. It wasn't until my health journey developed that I began to value my mental wellbeing, self-care and connection with nature.

Once again my life took a turn and I became off-balance. Old trauma, wounds and deep feelings of unworthiness that I had pushed down began to surface. I looked for a new coping mechanism to try and deal with things happening in my life and the way I felt. This internal unsettledness led me to restricting the amount of food I ate, the portions growing smaller and smaller.

I shrank and became tiny, like those supposedly 'perfect' models I saw in magazines, but I was unwell. I didn't have friends, I didn't have hobbies and I always felt cold. I wasn't able to express my creativity, I lost touch with my family – and my period stopped (a medical condition called amenorrhea). I didn't recognise myself. I lost sight of the girl that was funny, caring, creative and energetic.

Eventually, I began to acknowledge that my mental health was suffering and that I needed help. It took a few months of wanting to change before I was actually ready. After some time of seeing a therapist, one day by the ocean the clouds parted, and I finally caught sight of the warrior woman hidden inside me (one of those visions I get). I felt how strong I was. My true self was buried deep under layers and layers, but she was there. This moment was when I felt like everything aligned and my heart reconnected with my mind. I was finally ready to start healing. I reconnected with my destiny, purpose life and mission. I was reminded of the woman I wanted to be. From that day on, I fought. Day after day, I showed up with courage through all of my darkness and fear. I was ready to get my life back. Healing became my priority. I went to psychology sessions, spent time in nature and began reading recovery blogs, books and podcasts.

Recovering from poor mental health or an eating disorder is a bumpy road. However, I like to view my past as experiences that were *essential for my transformation*. My passion to learn, grow and heal has influenced me to study yoga, meditation, personal training and the psychology of eating. My fight to live the life I dream of is what has fuelled my fire to write this book!

Many healthy habits can produce immediate results, but some healing can take a long time. For example, it took me a few years of hard work to get my menstrual cycle functioning again. Stay committed and your efforts will pay off in the long term, believe me!

AMENORRHEA

If you experience amenorrhea (absent menstruation), please seek medical help as it can lead to further health complications. There can be many causes of amenorrhea, such as medical conditions, medications, hormone imbalances, pregnancy and menopause. However lifestyle factors like low body weight, excess stress or over-exercising can also cause amenorrhea.

Healing Past the Image

Evolving as a young person in this world, we can feel pressure from outside sources to fit into particular confines such as a size, look or aesthetic. This pressure can influence us into feelings of inadequacy or unworthiness and these are downright nasty feelings. The majority of us will have felt the pressure to alter our image at some point in our lives, maybe seeking an ideal of 'perfection'.

I hope you understand that the images created by a media-driven society are not reality. We see images of people in the media after filters have been applied, sometimes even body-resizing filters – what you're seeing isn't real. The most beautiful thing you can be is yourself. It is time to take a step out of the box – to see beyond labels, images and unrealistic aesthetics.

Spending time connecting with your heart and soul will enrich your life more than any amount of money, status or drive for the 'perfect' body. When I first began my self-love quest and chose to rebel against all the conditioning I'd placed on myself, I plastered the words 'FUCK PERFECT!' anywhere and everywhere. As I have evolved over the years, my views have changed and now I can see a reflection of perfection in my authentic natural state. It doesn't matter if you're a girl that likes to preach 'fuck perfect!' or if you can see perfection in everything and everyone. What matters is that your views serve you positively.

Body image and self-love are not things that we can change or fix overnight. But the more you can open up and surrender to the healing process, the easier it will be.

Energy
and Flow

According to Taoist philosophy, everything in this world has both Yin ('feminine') and Yang ('masculine') energy. Masculine and feminine can often be related to gender, but in this context I am speaking about universal energy and not referring to gendered categories. However you identify, whatever pronouns you use and whoever you are, both Yin and Yang energy exist within you. There could be potential for you to embrace the more masculine or feminine energy in order to create harmony.

Yin is represented in the divine feminine by naturalness, nourishment, flow and feeling. This feminine energy is what lies deep within the external body or the mask. One of the key healing practices I learned about while studying the psychology of eating was that, when there is a struggle with body image present, embracing the feminine is often key to creating harmony in the mind, body and soul. This Yin energy is about feeling content as you are.

When we lose touch with our feminine energy, we can become restricted and tight. This imbalance can manifest in our body and health in many ways, such as poor body image, stress and undesirable habits and behaviours like binge eating or drinking, shopping addiction or excess use of social media.

In the past, feminine expression was represented with greater respect for these soft, nourishing Yin-like qualities. Modern masculine qualities are defined by things such as how much money you have, how successful you are in your job and what your life looks like on paper. In modern society, with the growing influence of the media, we can feel pressured to be more masculine by being expected to look, live and work in a particular way. When we lose touch with our feminine nature, we can lose our truth and become off-balance.

There's a place for both Yin and Yang, but when there's negativity towards body image and food it's good to check in to make sure you are not stuck living in the energy of the masculine. This type of energy can be found in the modern world when we hear things like 'don't be emotional' or 'suck it up'. A domination of masculine energy can leave us feeling downright shit and trapped, reducing ourselves to narrow definitions, such as skinny, pretty or beautiful. We are so much more than that.

We all have feminine energy inside us, some of us more than others, and the truth of the feminine is emotional, delicate and soft.

I want to remind you to embrace your feelings. Feeling our emotions connects us with our inner essence and meaning. Embracing change and fluidity can help us to move away from emphasising the outer form. Know that it's okay to fluctuate. It's natural to be emotional, soft and changing and this doesn't correlate with weakness. Vulnerability is strength and tuning into feelings can help us get closer to our why. Every part of you is welcome.

Now might be a good time to do an inventory to find out if you have one energy overpowering the other. An excess of Yang (masculine) energy can often leave us wrapped up in external images and accomplishments. This may cause us to feel frustrated or stressed, or we may have trouble relaxing or difficultly expressing and feeling our emotions. Some things that can help bring in more Yin (feminine) energy are:

- implementing more fluidity in your diet and routine
- slow self-care practices
- resting
- embracing emotions
- journalling
- creating art
- eating cooling foods such as fruits and veggies.

An excess of Yin (feminine) energy may present us with symptoms such as lethargy, feeling cold and a lack of motivation. To bring in more Yang energy you could look at:

- implementing more structure
- setting goals
- trying a competitive sport
- using clear communication
- setting boundaries

- lifting weights (safely)
- building heat by eating heavier foods such as protein, cooked root veggies and spices.

If you want to learn more about the Yin and Yang energies, I recommend checking out studies of traditional Chinese medicine and Taoist philosophy.

FINDING FLOW

It took me a while to find fluidity in my lifestyle and health. When I was studying the psychology of eating – due to my mission to help others as well as myself – I began learning and implementing new practices into my life, and I went through periods of sticking to strict rules and regulations, such as particular workout plans or rigid ways of eating and living. After a short time, I always started to feel off-balance. Once I learned about the truth of the feminine (Yin), I understood why I needed to embrace more of that energy. The rigidity of my routines influenced me to lose my sense of flow, nourishment and dance.

The body is a system, therefore if we are tight in one aspect of our lives or health, it will have an impact on other parts of our wellbeing. When I ate like a robot, I didn't feel creative and free. I felt restricted. This is when I learned the importance of balance and flow. Life changes and evolves every day, and you should allow yourself to twist and turn with it.

We are all different, so it's important to find what works for you. For me, balance means taking some knowledge from diets, workout plans or structured lifestyle habits, but always making sure I listen to my body's needs. I find a way of living that allows me to feel free.

Body Image Is a State of Mind

'Nothing can survive
without food, including love.'

– The Buddha

This subject is powerful and I encourage you to approach it with curiosity, non-judgement and a positive attitude. Body image means essentially how you imagine your body. I want to bring to your attention the key word *imagine*. THAT'S RIGHT. Body image is a state of mind. The way you view your body can be positive, negative or neutral. However, no matter what shape, size or height your body is, you are enough as you are. If you lack feelings of self-worth, the most courageous thing you can do is to begin to heal your self-image. Although you already are enough, you just need to believe it. A healthy body image is when we accept and love the body that we are in.

SOME NOTES ON LOVE

The word 'love' represents our greatest gift as human beings. Love encompasses all. Every time I lose love, I feel like I've drifted off course in life. To me, love is the constant practice of staying open and trying not to let bad experiences or the winds of the world dim my light.

The Buddha speaks about the way love needs to be fed. It is not something that can be left on a shelf for years. I believe love needs to be a practice of checking in with yourself and asking what your heart is calling for. Is it craving to be fed and watered with acceptance? Do you need to release feelings of lacking or unworthiness? Does it require healing from a past relationship?

If you have lost trust in love for whatever reason, I want to remind you that love is the greatest gift on earth. No matter what has happened in your past or where you are in this moment, love does not wish to hurt you. Its nature is pure and whole. The more we can practise returning to a place of love, the more expansive and joyous we can feel.

No positive growth or long-term success will ever come from a place of negativity or hate. To begin to evolve we first have to love and accept where we are right now. Humans thrive on love, compassion and acceptance. Working towards a place of deep love and gratitude for your body is what can set you free. You don't need to dislike your body anymore. No matter what it looks or feels like, you can begin to work on accepting yourself just as you are.

HEALTHY BODY IMAGE

Transforming the way you view your body can transform your life. The law of vibration states that anything that exists in this universe is resonating on a particular frequency. Therefore, if I am moving through the world with a negative perception that resonates toxic beliefs, then the world will mirror this back to me and make things extremely difficult to change. This is how we can get stuck. If we are walking around with toxic thoughts about our body, the negative vibration can hold us back from creating the life we desire.

Every day we are bombarded with images from the media that influence us to believe we need to look a particular way. But guess what?! You hold the power to *reimagine* your body image, to change your state of mind and to feel content with the body you have, using the following steps as a guide.

Step 1

Observe the way you view your body. Use mindfulness to gain an understanding of your perception by acknowledging and getting to know the barriers and dislikes you have about your body.

Ask questions such as these.

- How do I view this body?
- Do I see myself as beautiful, sweet, loving and wonderful, or unwanted and strange?
- What is this energy I give to my body?
- Is the ideal of how I want my body to be making me suffer? (For example, I want to be a size 6 but this goal is restricting my life, making me feel anxious and isolated.)

If your answers uncover a negative relationship or bring up sadness and resistance, it's time to dig deeper. It's important to not hide from the things you don't like. We can choose to hide from our image, not look in the mirror and avoid seeing ourselves naked. However, one can only run from reality for so long, and this avoidance is more problematic and exhausting than doing the work itself. You *don't* need to put your life on hold. Observing and embracing your body can be scary, but it's never as bad as you imagine.

Step 2

Reinvent and reimagine the way you view your body. Think about it … every invention on our planet started with the imagination. We can plant the seed to create a more loving, healthy body image. It's time to become a cheerleader for yourself when it comes to internal self-talk. Sometimes it takes just that small change of dialogue to begin the journey of feeling good in your skin. It all starts within. For example, if you want to feel better in your body, can you begin to use positive self-talk to create an internal dialogue that is compassionate or uplifting? You can do this by using words that express gratitude for your body or boost your confidence. Remember, it's important to not aim too high too soon, though. Meet yourself at your individual stage of growth.

Don't shy away from things you don't like about your body. Try to have compassion and even gratitude for these features. They all make up who you are. For years I hid the hyperpigmentation scars on my legs. It felt stressful. Once I accepted them, they stopped bothering me and I felt more confident and empowered. It may feel scary at first, but you can slowly build peace with the parts of yourself you're struggling with. You can choose how to view your body and you can start to change the dialogue today.

- Love and embrace yourself.
- Create positive affirmations around your body.
- Have an attitude of gratitude!

We need to get back to our source and birthright as human beings. Think about babies and children. They rejoice in their physical form, embracing long limbs or chubby rolls. Improving body image is about getting back to our truth of lightness in the physical form.

Step 3

When we have a negative perception of parts of our bodies, we often 'disembody'. Disembodiment is when we are essentially 'checked out' of the body. This can be triggered by fear, trauma, past experiences or feelings of unworthiness. Fear of feeling can also leave us wanting to disembody, because the body stores a magnitude of feelings! When we disembody, we lose a connection to the source. This source is being in the body. We need to be in the body to begin to heal and work towards loving it.

Embodiment is about getting back into the body and building a connection that fosters feelings of empowerment. Try activities such as spending time in nature, dancing, yoga or any other exercise that you *love* and enjoy. Even just caring for your body by moisturising it can help you get back in touch with it.

Another simple way to embody is ... *feeling all the feelings*. Yes! It is essential to let yourself feel and express yourself. At some stage you may have been told to 'not be so emotional', but feeling is a gift. Suppressing emotions can cause imbalances in the body. A practice of embodiment is to welcome your feelings, good or bad – sit with them and then let them pass.

You look as good as you feel

☆

Movement

Movement is my medicine. My core motivation to move each day is because it makes me feel good on all levels. If used the right way, movement can help you feel empowered, confident, energetic and connected with your body, as well as enhance your mental clarity and improve your sleep. However, like all good things, if it is overused, it can cause imbalance.

I've been through many varied relationships with exercise, from overtraining to not moving my body at all. Luckily, all the trial and error has led me to a connection with movement that enhances my overall wellbeing.

- Having a six-pack will never make you happy if you don't do the inner mindwork.
- Your training should enhance your lifestyle, not take away from it.

- Listening to your body's unique movement needs is key to long-term success.
- Finding ways of moving that you enjoy is essential.
- Hitting the gym for an hour but not moving for the rest of the day won't give you many health benefits.
- Your daily posture, movement and activity as a whole is more important than any workout.
- No external goal can make up for a lack of self-love.

WHY MOVE?

If you want more energy, finding the right kind of exercise and moving your body will give you more energy! Movement also creates positive endorphins. When I am moving, inspiration flows and it helps me to think with more clarity, enriches my soul, boosts my brain health, supports my bowel health, helps me sleep better and inspires me to eat good-quality food.

There is some amazing research that shows the impact exercise can have on treating depression. One study included 30 moderately depressed people who were randomly assigned to different treatment groups. Those in the exercise intervention group experienced a greater relief from all symptoms of depression than those who were prescribed other treatment plans. The benefits of exercise can also be seen in the long term. Another study indicated that one year after a 12-week depression intervention exercise program, participants had maintained a reduction in anxiety and improved mood.

When it comes to sleep, exercise can increase the body's need for recovery, resulting in better sleep quality. However, intense exercise too close to bedtime can increase body temperature, cortisol levels and heart rate, making it hard to fall asleep. Therefore, I recommend opting for low to moderate-intensity exercise in the evenings. Save the hard workouts for during the day.

UPGRADE YOUR MOVEMENT

You don't have to work out or go to the gym to upgrade your movement. Just try sitting less and standing more. Can you get a stand-up desk at work or home? Could you add more steps into your day? For example, take a break to jog around the block, use the stairs instead of the lift, or choose to walk up that hill instead of drive to get your coffee or lunch. Can you do squats when you get up from your desk to use the bathroom, or while waiting for the kettle to boil?

FIND YOUR JAM

Test out different types of exercise until you find things that you love and make you feel good. Yoga, running, weight lifting, swimming, walking, dancing … the possibilities are endless. There is no point doing things you don't enjoy because they will not stick long term. Of course, starting new habits can be hard at first, but when you feel the ways they positively impact your life, they will become things you crave doing. If you find types of exercise you love, moving your body will become an ingrained part of your lifestyle. It's a good idea to get a movement screening carried out by a fitness professional when beginning a new program. If you are new to weight lifting, it's essential to get advice on the correct form and technique. If you have joint or muscle pain or weakness, always seek help from a professional.

There are many different types of exercise. Personal trainers create personalised programs for strength, power, speed and agility, cardiovascular endurance, flexibility, balance and coordination. I like to keep things simple and break up the types of exercise into four main forms.

- **Strength** – weight lifting or strength training with machine assistance, weights or bodyweight.
- **Aerobic** – cardio exercise such as walking, running, cycling, swimming and dance.

- **High-Intensity Interval Training (HIIT)** – cardio exercise or a mix of high-intensity strength and cardio.
- **Flexibility/Balance** – such as tai chi and yoga.

- High-intensity exercise can be detrimental to your health if you already have a high-stress lifestyle.
- High-intensity exercise can stimulate the stress hormone cortisol, and high cortisol levels can cause irritability, weight gain, insulin resistance and can affect concentration.

STRENGTH TRAINING

Weight and resistance training has been a part of my lifestyle for years. I love lifting weights because it helps me to feel strong and empowered. During my mental-health recovery, a combination of therapy and strength training drastically improved my mental wellbeing. The gym was a space that positively impacted my recovery.

So, why prioritise strength training?

- It increases our fast-twitch muscle fibres, which are associated with an overall reduction in body mass.
- It protects us from the wear and tear of ageing.
- It improves metabolic function.
- It prevents injuries.
- It can reduce the risk of disease and early death (due to a greater retention of muscle mass).

LIMITATIONS

Sometimes we can get caught up in stereotypes of what a 'good' athlete looks like or can do. Do you have a particular idea in your head of a runner, swimmer or cyclist? Or do you think that if something isn't easy the first few times you try it, that you simply just aren't 'built' for it? These thoughts are often stereotypes or false perceptions. You will definitely be able to find something that you love and that suits your body, no matter what shape, size or age you are, whether it's running, dancing, yoga, walking or *anything* you want. It's likely that the only limitations are the ones you have on yourself. Now is a great time to check in with yourself. Don't let the monkey mind – the non-stop chattering, distracting part of the mind – stop you. Practise positive thinking and ask questions to find out if your perceptions are realities or simply limitations. Of course, if you have any underlying health conditions, you have to respect these, but you will still be able to find something that suits you.

HOW EXERCISE IMPROVED MY MENTAL HEALTH

Training for my first half marathon was one of the most powerful decisions I made on my road to recovery from under-fuelling my body. At the time, I was not aware of the way it would help me heal. Since the age of 16, running has always been my favourite type of movement. During my modelling years while battling with my mental health, I mistreated running. I ran like a robot – always the same distance and route. If I was tired, I forced myself to run.

Once I started to heal, my mental state became clearer and I took a big, hard look at my life. I took an inventory of all the habits and practices that had flowed through my life. I asked myself the following questions.

- What can help me on my road to recovery?
- What is a practice that I can show up and do every day – to keep me accountable on this healing journey – with the intention of improving my life?

My intuition led me to running at sunrise. I knew it needed to be something I could do early in the morning – also, sunrise appealed to me because the sky is different every day, so that added a layer of excitement. I lived 10 minutes from the beach and I was always thrilled when I rounded the corner every morning to see what epic colours were waiting for me. (Also, the sun rises every day, so that kept me accountable!) I set my intention on using this practice, along with psychology sessions in my initial recovery, to support me and remind me of my strength.

Months on, my life had taken a turn. The simple practice of 'running the rise' brought magic into my life. As the mornings passed, my running and motivation began to improve. I wanted to get faster and I craved being able to run huge hills, so I signed up for my first half marathon. I wanted to be the person that could start a Sunday morning with a 15-kilometre run. I love racing, and I love having a specific event to train for. That's just me, it might not be for you.

The drive to improve in running also improved my relationship with food. I began to love fuelling my body. I would choose to eat a nourishing meal so that my running performance would benefit. I knew that if I skimped on my nutrition, there was no way I was going to improve.

My positive intention to use a simple practice such as running to keep me accountable for my mental health was a huge step in my recovery. I was on a journey of rediscovery, following my values and beliefs. Doing things – big and small – every day to become the person I had always dreamed of being.

RUNNING

I often write love stories about running. This might sound a bit extra, but this powerful practice supports and inspires me. There are no mirrors; there is no competition from others; it's a space that allows me to feel free, where my mind can wander. It's my jam, and I do it often. I run because it makes me feel happy. This is my *why* for running and the reason why I show up every day to move.

Did you know that running can have psychological benefits and is often compared to the treatment of psychotherapy? A 'runner's high' is caused by a couple of things: a rush of endorphins that act on the opioid receptors in the brain; and endocannabinoids, a naturally occurring biochemical substance that acts on the brain's pleasure centres, producing that post-run bliss.

Running has positively influenced my life in many ways. If you have no interest in taking up running, that's fine, but if you are excited at the idea of becoming a runner, I can tell you what I've learned along the way.

When beginning, you will more than likely have a few days where your legs feel tired and heavy before experiencing the greatness of a run that sends goosebumps down your spine. A commitment to consistency is essential. Showing up for yourself time and time again. What at first takes effort will soon become your lifestyle. To be honest, after a few months off I feel like shit on my first two weeks back into running, but once you break through the wall, it's *epic*. The problem is that most people give up in the first week. But nothing great ever came from giving up. I've found that sticking with things brings great results and happiness. Be dedicated to the process and you will reap the rewards.

This is your life and committing to living a great one asks you to keep showing up. There has never been a moment in my life where I have regretted going for a run, even if it's only a few minutes. Every day, I get the opportunity to lace up my runners, set my intention and move. If you find a movement practice that resonates with you, you will hopefully feel the same.

Discover what you enjoy doing and, during the initial stages of creating a habit around this movement, make a promise to do it – even on the hard days. Enjoy the process. Relish in all the good. Back yourself, baby! And remember, it doesn't matter what exercise someone else does – they are not you. Your individual flair requires a form of movement that is unique to you and your body.

My Health Tips on Movement:

- With all the life-enhancing benefits that exercise can have, I recommend moving first thing in the morning or before lunchtime to reap the benefits of greater mental clarity, better food choices, improved mood and focus and an increase in energy throughout your day. A study published by the *Psychological Bulletin* found a correlation between exercise and increased energy, even with those suffering from a medical condition. Furthermore, more than 90 per cent of other studies report the same improvement that movement has on fatigue.
- If you run or work out with music, try to spend the last 10 minutes of your session without sound blasting in your ears. In Ben Greenfield's book *Boundless: Upgrade Your Brain, Optimize Your Body & Defy Aging*, he states that this will help to calm the nervous system and stop excess sensory stress.

KEEP THINGS BALANCED

There are two sides to every story. As with everything, sometimes we can get out of balance. Movement should uplift your life, not control or limit it. In the past, I experienced an unhealthy relationship with training. I used exercise as a distraction to avoid my feelings.

Some beautiful things happened when I finally let go. I started to hang out with my friends more. I had more time and energy to pour into other things. I discovered my love for writing. I began to read books and create art. It can be scary to loosen your grip on the tools that offer you distraction, but take your time – it's worth it. If you have an unhealthy relationship with exercise, I understand, because I was there too. But the love of life I have gained from creating balance has made me a happier person.

If sport is your career or you are training for a specific sporting event that sets your soul on fire and you need to spend hours training, then *amazing* – go kill it. But if you are spending hours in the gym or exercising for other reasons, it could be time to ask yourself *why*.

Following are some important questions you can ask yourself about your relationship with movement.

- Do your exercise habits come before family, friends, passions, etc?
- Do you need more movement in your life, or do you need less of it?
- Do you feel like a failure if you don't move enough?
- Are your movement practices positively impacting your health – body, mind and spirit?
- Is your relationship with exercise coming from feelings of unworthiness?
- Do you work out to simply burn energy?

If the answers to these questions spark feelings of imbalance in your relationship to exercise, it might be a good time to talk to someone you trust. You can ask for help or maybe start to challenge your behaviours by hanging out with friends more, or slowly cutting down your exercise time. If your answers revealed that you don't move enough, maybe plan some exercise dates with your friends.

Exercise should be what you enjoy. However, it shouldn't define you. When I suffered from a hip injury and lost my ability to train, my sense of identity and world crumbled. Not being able to move made me realise that I had let my athletic capabilities become my identity. Those days had me asking big questions such as: *Who am I if I am not fit? What is the real identity of Isabelle?*

MOVEMENT MOTIVATION 101

If you are struggling with motivation to exercise, you could go back and work through the Setting Goals and Staying Motivated chapter in Part 1 of the book (page 80). Here are some other ways to get out of thick motivation mud.

Find Movement You Enjoy – If you find something that you enjoy doing, you will feel more easily motivated to do it. Experiment and try different ways of moving until you discover what you love.

Know Your Reasons Why – Ask yourself some questions to get clarity on why movement has a positive effect on your life. Continually remind yourself of these reasons.

Set Goals – Set fitness and movement goals, and create rewards for your work. I like to start with my end goal and work backwards from there. Don't forget to try the SMART goal-setting formula on page 81.

Be Consistent – Consistency is the key to success. What at first takes a lot of effort will soon become your lifestyle. The initial few weeks of any new habit will bring resistance, but that's normal. Think about your epic life and long-term goals. Commit to the journey and the process.

Enhance Your Chance of Success – Make workout playlists you love. Recruit a training buddy or a friend to walk with. Sign up for a fitness challenge or race, or join a new group exercise class. Create a training journal to express how you feel before and after exercise.

The mind may tell you to quit before the body is ready. Time and time again when I am on a run, I will notice thoughts that tell me to stop. If I ignore the first few thoughts, often they don't come back. This has allowed me to move through the initial wall of resistance and normal discomfort while exercising.

POSITIVE SELF-TALK

Positive self-talk in relation to training has helped me to make breakthroughs in movement motivation. When I am on a run and need support, I give myself encouragement.

- You can do it, Iz!
- You've got this!
- Think about how epic you'll feel afterwards.

Create a slogan that you can say to yourself when you need motivation, such as 'consistency is the key to success' or 'growth is growth, no matter how small'. Try some different positive self-talk slogans and see what you vibe with.

You don't have to fall into a failure formula. Believe you can do it, and you're halfway there. Your mind is a powerhouse, and you can achieve what you want. Make the decision to put in the work and keep fighting for what you want. Know your reasons *why* and continually remind yourself of your goals. Have the courage to break through the resistance wall of the initial few weeks and back yourself! You've got this.

DANCE

When uncomfortable feelings arise for me, movement is my medicine. I breathe and dance. I connect with my body and express myself physically. When I feel stuck or hit resistance in my mind, I move. All my mind clutter vanishes and I feel a sense of freedom and connection to my body.

One afternoon in Los Angeles, I was scrolling through my iPhone and came across a video of a person wildly dancing in their underwear. They radiated so much liberty and joy. I had just finished an acting class and the project I was working on was quite traumatic. I'd walked home to get some fresh air, but I was still struggling to shake off the bad vibes. The dancing video affected my mindset, creating a ripple effect that made me laugh incredibly hard. Next thing I knew, I was in the living room blasting music and dancing like crazy. It was incredible. The dance was like therapy. It allowed all the stagnant energy to leave my body, and I felt so free and connected.

From that day, dance has been a huge part of my mental, physical and spiritual health. When I find myself in a negative headspace, dancing completely transforms my attitude. Over the past few years, I have visited dance therapy classes and an array of sober dance parties. My last sober day dance party was in an underground nightclub, glitter undies and sparkles included.

There is nothing like expressing how I'm feeling through dance. For years, I was in disbelief of my ability to express through this kind of movement. I craved nights out boogieing, but I was scared. I had a false perception that I needed to be a 'dancer' to dance.

>>

I now know that the power of dance can be harvested anywhere anytime, no clubs needed. If you are not physically able to dance, I recommend substituting this type of movement with breathwork or meditation to music.

Everyone can dance, including you! It's just about getting out of your own way and letting yourself express and move without judgement. You don't have to be a 'dancer'. You don't have to have experience on the d-floor. All you need to do is put on some music and move. There are no rules or regulations, hell you don't even need to use dance moves. The other day I came out with some weird ballet/contemporary shit I had no idea even existed in me. It was fun!

I also use the power of dance to move through my emotions. It's okay to feel whatever arises when you dance. Some days, dance expression might shake up some uncomfortable feelings, other days, it may bring up pure joy. Everything you feel is valid. Emotions arise to be felt, and once felt, they can be released. Dress up or don't. Dance outside or dance alone in your bedroom. Book into dance classes or try a sober dance party. The possibilities are endless! The simple practice of dance can enhance your wellbeing in so many ways. So just remember to DANCE, baby.

The Butterfly Effect

'The Butterfly Effect' is a theory that describes how one small change can serve as a catalyst for greater events – that the tiny beat of a butterfly wing can cause a storm on the other side of the world. This theory inspired me. I have felt first-hand the way one positive action ripples into my day, my week and life. Can you begin your day with one simple habit or action that can create a positive ripple? It doesn't matter what you choose, what matters is that you try. For example, if you can devote just 5 minutes when you wake to meditate, set a 'happy' intention for the day, or do some journalling, the positive benefits will flow into the rest of your day. Mornings are the perfect time to start cultivating change. And if you 'mess up' and miss one day, that's okay. Just pick yourself up and try again tomorrow.

A SIMPLE EXERCISE FOR WHEN YOU'RE FEELING STUCK

You can use the power of the butterfly effect if you ever feel stuck or challenged.

- Create three action words. These words are the top things you need to prioritise to get back on track.
- Write a list of the actions and complete them to start a positive flow-on effect. The first one needs to be the most basic. For example:

  1. Make my bed.
  2. Go for a walk without my phone.
  3. Plan out my week.

Each of these actions is a catalyst for moving forward. A critical step is making sure your first few actions are achievable and realistic. Don't choose things you doubt you can complete, because this can set you up for further disappointment – this is why we start small and easy.

Visualise yourself getting back on track. Create the upcoming day and week in your mind and see yourself living it. How will you feel? What will you do? Feel free to write down in your journal some things you want to do for the week ahead.

Okay, now you are done with the serious stuff – time to shake it off and do something fun.

Shake It Up

Look at your day or week and find some space to plan an
activity just for you. Something that's different and fun,
because having fun is a great way to remove stress and
negative energy. I like to shake things up on the regular.
Trying new things to *let go* helps me keep a zest for life. You
could start by playing some music and dancing wildly, or
maybe it is the week for you to try surfing, playing
basketball with a friend or making jewellery (my fave).

Life is life, and it can sometimes throw us curve balls. In these
times, I try to remember that it doesn't matter what I haven't been
doing, what matters is what I am about to *start* doing. There is no use
beating yourself up. After honouring your feelings, it's important not
to sit in the 'victim' or 'poor me' mindset for too long. Accept where
you are and take a small step to break the pattern. Then, let that one
initial positive action bring a sequence of uplifting events. The rut is
just a temporary state, and it can be transformed.

*Your new life starts with
just one small step*

♡

HEALTHY HABIT PAIRING

Healthy habit pairing is essentially practising one healthy habit, then following it up with a second one that rides the wave created by your first positive habit. For example, my favourite healthy habit pairing is running followed by meditation. If I go for a run, I meditate for 10 minutes afterwards. Pairing the habits makes them feel effortless.

When beginning this health journey, you may find it beneficial to try healthy habit pairing. There are many possibilities, but make sure to customise your habits to your needs. For example, you may like to pair earthing (being barefoot in nature) with a few minutes of journalling.

The things we do each day become our habits. A study published by Duke University in 2006 showed that 40 per cent of the tasks people did each day were not decisions but habits.

MIND TIP

When things get a little shitty, I ask myself, *How would my higher self deal with this situation?* I like to view my 'higher self' as the wise me – the part of me that is connected to my heart, happiness and wellbeing. The other voice inside my head is one that makes me feel bad, unworthy or tries to limit me. I like to view this as my 'small self' – the part of me that can be influenced to act based on external circumstances, my shadow or ego. I find that just asking the question directly to my higher self connects me with that space. I ask the question, say my answer out loud, listen to it and then make decisions and take action from that space.

ENJOY THE JOURNEY

Finish lines and end results are fabulous, but the journey is just as goddamn beautiful. Failing to enjoy the journey is like not stopping to smell the roses. Life is too short. We can get so caught up in the end results, believing that the finish line will offer a reward or gratification that we can not fulfil in the process. But we can find joy on the path, for the path ultimately becomes the result. The journey is where all the memories are made. It's where you grow and evolve. The process of working towards the goal can teach you more about yourself than any end result.

The journey is just as beautiful as the end goal.

AN IMPORTANT NOTE

My food philosophy has evolved from studying nutrition and the psychology of eating, and the tools I created and adapted to overcome my personal struggles. It's important to state that I am not a dietitian or health professional. This section is for people who might be caught in a cycle of eating junk or unsustainable dieting, or for those who were maybe never taught about nutrition and need some general advice and inspiration so they can improve their relationship with food. I've experienced first-hand the issues discussed here, so I'm going to share what I've learned.

Part 3
EAT WELL

My Food Philosophy

Diets suck and can leave you in the dust time and time again. I don't believe in diets. I believe in the power of healthy, flexible eating. Food doesn't have to cause you stress and worry. You can have food freedom, eat in abundance and feel amazing by building a positive relationship with food and eating as much real, whole food as possible. (While I don't believe in 'diets', if you have specific health conditions, like diabetes, food intolerances or allergies, you will probably need to develop a diet plan in consultation with an accredited practising dietitian or other healthcare professional.)

If your relationship with food is not good right now, don't worry ... you have the power to transform it! I know, because I've been there. As you build a healthier relationship with food, you will see how it can have a direct impact on your wellbeing. Try to stay open minded and curious about the links between your relationship with food and other parts of your lifestyle.

- No diet or food can fill a space that's lacking and craving self-love.
- Unwanted eating habits can signal that there is some imbalance in our life.
- Our relationship with food can have a link to our relationship with others. Restriction with food can mean a restriction is present in friendships or other relationships.

A HEALTHY RELATIONSHIP WITH FOOD

As we grow and evolve through life's ups and downs, our relationship with food can be rocked. But all of us have the power to build, or rebuild, a healthier relationship with food. Sometimes the work is not so much about *doing* but rather *undoing*. This means loosening our grip and freeing ourselves from toxic beliefs, such as feeling guilty about eating certain foods.

Once you add more of a mind–body eating philosophy into your lifestyle, I believe you will begin to feel more connected with your inner world. This connection will help support you by influencing your body to crave more nourishing food. Once you feel, see and experience the benefits of eating a more nutritious and flexible diet, you may find that your cravings for foods that don't make you feel your best start to minimise, then maybe even disappear.

I have struggled with my nutrition and experienced unwanted food habits, low energy and poor gut health. Years of trying to heal my symptoms by fixating on food led me nowhere. One day, I finally had the 'aha' moment I needed and realised that my relationship with food was connected to all the other parts of my life. By understanding this, my world shifted, and your world can shift with this realisation, too.

Everything in your body is connected. The ingredients in food can impact the way you think and the way your brain functions. I like to say, 'premium petrol for a premium tank'. For your brain to function at its full capacity, ideally you should provide it with optimal hydration, vitamins, minerals and nutrients. Have you noticed that after an indulgent meal (or many), you feel cloudy in the head, lethargic, unmotivated or low?

EATING WELL IS A PLEASURE

To me, eating well is never a hardship, but I see it as a gift that comes from having respect and love for my body. After a period of eating healthy foods, you may notice that you have clearer skin and a more radiant complexion. You may also see an improvement in brain function, memory and mental stamina. A healthy diet can also increase your energy, improve physical capabilities and aid muscle recovery. When compared to processed foods, wholefoods contain more vitamins, nutrients, fibre and water (great for post-exercise rehydration). Healthy fats can also help to minimise muscle inflammation. Eating nutritious food can improve your sleep and reduce your risk of disease. A diet rich in plant foods has even been shown to increase the average human lifespan! For information on great foods to include in your diet, see Eat to Nourish on page 137.

I believe that if you eat real food as often as you can, respect your body and its desires, and prioritise nutrition for the mind *and* body, you will thrive.

We are bombarded with different diets, such as low carb, low fat, low salt, pescatarian, etc. However, UCLA research shows that the majority of restrictive diets fail. A sustainable approach to food is one that *you* create and that works for *you*. I encourage you to focus on eating as best you can but not limiting yourself to ideals such as 'clean eating'. Labels like 'clean' may suggest that other foods are 'not clean' which can trigger feelings of shame and guilt about food choices.

We can waste so much energy starting new restrictive diets, but we're rarely warned about how difficult it is to come off them. If you follow strict rules or regulations, there will always be a moment when life events or your body's cravings get in the way. Confining yourself to rules can be a recipe for disaster for some people. Coming off a restrictive diet can leave you with feelings of guilt, regret, confusion, anxiety and stress. It's feelings like these that we are trying to avoid if we want a healthy relationship with food.

But guess what? You are allowed to eat in a way that is unique to *you*. Ditch the restrictive diets and ditch the labels. Listen to your body's wisdom and refuse to let your mind and intuition get clouded by advertising and false promises. Working on practices that help you create a positive relationship with food will sustain you in the long term.

✷ *Prioritise real food*

✷ *Build a positive food relationship*

✷ *Nourish yourself*

Why Eat 'Healthy'?

'Healthy' can be a loaded word, but its context here is about finding a balanced diet that serves you and your body and helps you live your best life. Your nutritional needs are individual and influenced by factors like your age, gender, genetics, culture, how much you move, work and sleep, where you live, what season it is and, of course, your overall health. No one way of eating works for everyone.

As children, we have natural likes and dislikes when it comes to food. We have not yet been programmed, influenced or impacted by information, other people's opinions, external influences, physical pressure or nutritional facts. We eat when we are hungry, and sometimes we eat more and other times less. Food and nutrition are dictated by the wisdom and instinct of the body.

My motivation to eat well comes from my *why*. I ask myself: *Why should I eat fresh fruit and vegetables? Why should I prioritise a positive relationship with food?* The answer to both questions is that eating 'real' food transformed my life and health and continues to benefit me every day. (By 'real' I mean food that's as close to its natural state as possible.) Before I learned to navigate my emotions, I used to eat packets of junk food, lollies and frozen meals. When I became interested in nutrition, I started making healthy swaps. My palate began to change, and I began to have an increase in mental and physical energy. My skin began to glow, my eyes were brighter, I slept better and I experienced fewer energy crashes. My mind became clearer which then positively affected my mood and mindset.

I considered the 'butterfly effect', and how thinking big and small might help. I started with small swaps. I added health-boosting things here and there, such as chia seeds and blueberries in a smoothie. Every time I ran out of something in my pantry, I'd try and replace it with something that might fuel me better – coconut yoghurt instead of dairy, veggie pasta instead of wheat, nut mix instead of dried fruit mixes. Small changes like these can all add up to a bigger change in your overall health.

If you are someone who can eat whatever you like and still keep your desired body weight or type, then I want to bring to your attention that *it's not just about the external, but the internal too.* The body is more complex than that. Thinking about energy or fuel in the form of calories alone is a big mistake. The body responds very differently to 500 calories of vegetables compared to 500 calories of fries. If we want to experience true internal health, we need to try and remove these unhelpful beliefs around food.

We can be limited by the toxic thought that healthy eating is only about weight loss or achieving the 'perfect' body. However, improving your relationship with food and eating more healthy foods (see page 137) is a great step to becoming the best version of yourself and to help you live a life of vitality and joy. Let's try and fill our bodies and minds with as much good stuff as we can.

Each mealtime is an opportunity. If you eat food that has a positive vibration from its nutritional value, then you can gain positive vibrations in return. I bring my mind and body into alignment when making food choices. Before I eat, I will often ask myself questions such as: *What am I craving? What real foods can I add to this meal? What foods are going to make me feel my best?*

A wholefoods diet can support your body in ways such as improving immune function, mental health, blood sugars, overall wellbeing and decreasing risk of disease. Plant-based foods have also been shown to help the immune system with their higher concentrations of fibre, vitamins, nutrients and antioxidants.

Relax and Trust

1. Relax – Relaxation is potent metabolic magic, and I will remind you of its power time and time again. Stress puts the body into a fight-or-flight response, which essentially tells the body to tighten and shut down. This stress chemistry impacts the body by putting it into digestive shutdown, leading to nutrient excretion and fat storage.

2. Trust Your Body – You hold the wisdom. Once you have a basic understanding of what healthy foods are, and what makes your body feel great, then you can stop stressing about all that outside distraction and conflicting information and trust your body.

Eat to Nourish

Eating to nourish yourself is not a 'diet'. It does not have to come with unbreakable rules and regulations. It is about including as many nutrient-rich foods in your diet as often as possible. If you want to start eating more nourishing foods but are confused about all the nutrition advice out there, this chapter contains some information that may help you. Of course, you need to find what works for you and your body, but below are some of my favourite nourishing foods.

WHOLEFOODS

Wholefoods that are in their most natural state come from the earth. They're foods that come in an array of colours and are as fresh, in season and as locally sourced as possible. I'm talking about food that has not been tampered with, such as (preferably organically grown) fruits, vegetables, nuts, seeds, legumes, beans, grains and small amounts of animal proteins (if you are not eating a solely plant-based diet). The more variety, the better, as different colours provide different nutrients, vitamins and minerals. As the saying goes about eating a balanced diet, 'eat the rainbow'!

CARBOHYDRATES

Yes, carbohydrates! Healthy carbohydrates come from sources such as wholegrains and starches. I'm talking rice, sweet potato, potato, pumpkin, quinoa, fruits, legumes, buckwheat, oats and other yummy, nutritious sources. I prefer wholegrain, low-GI or high-fibre breads, pasta and cereals.

PROTEINS

Protein sources that come from plants, animals or fish, and are as close to nature as possible, are ideal. If you choose to eat animal products, make sure they are from quality sources. Look for labels such as organic, grass-fed, pasture-raised and wild-caught. Nourishing plant protein can come from foods like beans, legumes, organic soy, hemp seeds and chia.

Eat the rainbow

Feel like the rainbow

HEALTHY FATS

Healthy unrefined fat sources include avocado, coconut, nuts, seeds and fish, as well as high-quality oils such as olive, sesame, coconut, almond and flaxseed.

GREENS

Load up on greens! They offer potent super-concentrated nutrition and are full of antioxidants, minerals and vitamins. Dark leafy greens such as kale and spinach also provide a nice amount of plant-based iron. The nutrients provided contribute to providing sustained energy for the body and may improve the health of your hair, skin, nails, digestion and more. I recommend adding greens to any meal or snack you can, such as salads, stir-fries, pasta dishes, smoothies and juices. If I'm travelling, I'll always pack a jar of powdered greens to mix into water and drink in the mornings or before a workout.

FIBRE

Fibre is fabulous and nourishes the gut and colon, which play a crucial role in our immune system, metabolism, mental health and energy. Fibre also satisfies hunger and I love to add a boost of it wherever I can. Some of my favourite natural fibre boosters are chia seeds, flaxseeds and psyllium husk. Fruits and veggies also contain loads of fibre, so make sure to load up on them. Hot tip for your tum: when adding these fibre boosters to your diet, do so gently and with an increase in water intake to avoid constipation – particularly with psyllium.

'Eat food. Not too much.
Mostly plants.'

– Michael Pollan

THINGS I TRY TO LIMIT OR AVOID

Foods with less nourishment include processed or refined products, food with artificial ingredients added, dairy (if you have an intolerance to it), gluten (if you have an intolerance to it), as well as sugary drinks and flavoured yoghurts.

One of my favourite doctors, Mark Hyman, says, 'Think of meat and animal products as condiments, or, as I like to call them, "condimeat" – not a main course. Vegetables should take centre stage, and meat should be the side dish.'

Unhealthy oils include vegetable oils or oils that have been processed with high heat. These oils will often be labelled as 'trans fats', so check labels for these and avoid. We need fats in our diet, but it's better for your wellbeing to choose the healthy ones.

Himalayan or Celtic sea salt are healthier alternatives to table salts, and making your own sauces and salad dressings, rather than using store-bought ones, are super-easy ways to avoid sugary sauces and ready-made salad dressings.

SUGAR

A diet that is higher in simple or refined sugars can have unfavourable health impacts. Processed sugar can spike blood-glucose levels in the body and disrupt the bacteria in the gut, creating digestive distress and potentially leading to problems like leaky gut.

By sugar, I don't mean the sugars found in fruits and veggies. I'm referring to other types, such as white and brown sugar, coconut sugar, agave and corn syrup (remember, it's about balance, so small amounts now and again are okay!). More natural sugars such as honey, rice malt syrup, maple syrup or dates are good alternatives but, with any form of sugar, I like to say 'everything in moderation'. For added nutritional benefits, I recommend trading out dried fruits for the fresh fruit instead. My favourite natural sugar-free sweeteners are stevia, monk fruit and erythritol.

DAIRY

A study called 'Milk and Health' published in the *New England Journal of Medicine* suggests that we don't actually need milk for our bones and we can get enough calcium from other foods. In fact, one serving of kale has around the same amount of calcium as one glass of milk. According to research by Walter Willett and David Ludwig, if you eat your greens and include foods such as chia seeds, almonds and tahini in your diet daily, your calcium intake should be adequate, but I always recommend to check with a health professional, such as a nutritionist or GP, if you are worried about your nutrient intake.

Dairy can be mucus-forming and may create a bile-like lining in the throat, gut and colon. I found that after removing dairy from my diet, I no longer have to clear my throat due to sticky mucus. These days, if I dabble in dairy, I feel the effects on my energy and digestion. The good thing is, there are many dairy alternatives. Some of my favourites are plant-based milks like coconut, almond or oat milk; cheeses made from nuts and seeds; and yoghurts made from almonds, cashews or coconut. It is really easy and fun to make nut milks and cheese at home! You might like to give these alternatives a try and see how your skin and digestive system respond.

WHAT ABOUT SOY?

Processed soy is often genetically modified and comes with the same health concerns as non-organic fruits, vegetables and meats. Organic, non-GMO is always a better option and, like anything, moderation is key.

CRAVINGS AND THE 80/20 RULE

Life is about enjoyment. I like to practise the 80/20 rule, as this is achievable and sustainable for me. It's where you eat nourishing foods 80 per cent of the time and 20 per cent is about eating flexibly to fulfil life's events, our desires or any food cravings.

When I eat wholefoods and make sure I am getting all my nutritional needs, my cravings for less-nourishing foods are not as frequent. My body now craves food such as cacao, homemade dark chocolate (with at least 70 per cent cocoa) or a creamy vanilla protein smoothie over items such as chocolate bars and ice cream.

- Nutrition is not as simple as energy in versus energy out.
- There is no perfect diet.

PLANT-BASED LIVING

I adopted a vegan diet at age 13, which I followed for 10 years. However, after recovering from my eating disorder, an essential value of my specific healing journey was to remove all the rules and regulations I had around food. So I started reintroducing dairy-free animal products to my diet, adding in wild-caught fish and then eggs and organic white meat. After a year of experimenting, I found a balance that helped me to feel my best, once again eating a plant-based diet. This decision was initially led by my body's wisdom. My blood panel results after a year of eating animal products also backed up what I was feeling. I was guided back to a plant-based diet, this time with no labels, rules or restrictions.

My body, skin, energy levels and digestion all thrive on a plant-based diet, and yours might too. I love to eat plant-based for my health, the environment and the animals. I like to say that you eat what the animal ate, so if you eat animal products, think about where they came from, as cheap meats can contain processed grains and hormones.

If you are eating a plant-based diet, it's beneficial to take an inventory of your diet to make sure you are hitting all your macronutrients. Try not to fall into a vegan diet of eating carbohydrate-only meals of bread. Carbs aren't to be avoided, but it's all about balance. Make sure you have plenty of greens and veggies on the same plate. Balancing carb meals with proteins and fats will keep your energy and mood stable.

If we eat enough of the right stuff, we should be able to get all our nutritional needs from food. Don't forget, I always suggest checking things over with a health professional to ensure you are meeting your dietary needs and they can recommend tailored supplements if required. If you're following a plant-based diet and lack energy, check in with your GP. They can order you some simple blood tests to see if you need an extra boost of essential nutrients such as iron or B_{12}. I make sure to take a B_{12} supplement, which is a common supplement for plant-based foodies. Personally, eating an abundance of plants provides me with stacks of energy to run and train and my blood panels are great. Your body is unique, though, so listen to it and adjust your diet accordingly.

If you are interested in adopting a plant-based diet, start small by including more veggies in meals than meats. Swap red meat for wild-caught fish or chicken, and then begin to swap animal products like dairy and eggs to plant-based alternatives such as chickpea scrambles and almond, oat or coconut milk. You don't have to rush the process. It's okay to have a gradual transition to a plant-based diet, as we're looking for sustainability in the long term. And guess what? It's totally okay if plant-based isn't for you, either! You don't need to eat a vegetarian or vegan diet to feel happy and healthy in your own skin. You just have to listen to your body and honour its needs.

My Healthy Hacks

In this chapter I want to share some tips and tricks that I've discovered on my journey of healthy eating. As well as general hacks and some tips on energy, hydration and digestion, I also include some notes about caffeine and alcohol.

LOW ON ENERGY?

If you find yourself struggling with low energy in the first half of the day, you could try lightening up your breakfast to fast-track your digestion. Choose foods that digest rapidly, such as fresh fruits, smoothies or veggies. Load up on fruit and veggies from all the colours of the rainbow, such as cucumber, tomatoes and blueberries. The process of digesting a complex meal uses energy. If you are doing a workout, your body requires as much energy as possible. Try to wait for 2 hours after a meal to work out or reach for a light snack such as fruit.

HYDRATE!

Your body is roughly 60 per cent water, so it's important to stay hydrated. Hydration status may impact your energy levels, sleep, skin, mood, digestion and overall wellbeing. If possible, opt for high-quality water, such as spring, purified, reverse osmosis or alkaline. Aim for at least 2 litres a day, depending on your body size and level of physical activity. It's beneficial to hydrate as much as you can throughout the day so you can drink less water in the evenings, as it can disrupt sleep. It's not about being perfect, but being conscious!

SHOPPING TIPS

When you're next at the supermarket, notice that you'll find the healthiest food around the outside edges of the aisles. I like to shop around the perimeter of the supermarket first, filling my trolley with all the good, real food, such as fresh vegetables, fruit and nuts etc. Before you go shopping, check what's in season as those fresh foods will be at their best, and probably cheapest too!

I also recommend shopping locally as much as possible, especially from farmers' markets. This way you know your food is fresh, as well as where it came from.

RAW CACAO

I like to call raw cacao 'God's food'. Unprocessed cacao, aka raw chocolate, comes from the cacao beans that grow on trees in hot climates. If you can't get access to cacao, organic cocoa is a great substitute. The difference is that it's not raw, therefore it doesn't contain as many vitamins and nutrients (or vibes).

I use raw cacao daily for a pre-workout pick-me-up or a homemade hot chocolate. High-quality forms of cacao are considered a natural plant medicine. The magic of cacao is used to heal and connect our mental, physical and spiritual bodies to each other. It's considered a 'love drug', and we all need more love. Not to mention, it is high in antioxidants as well as vitamins and minerals such as magnesium and sulphur.

Raw cacao benefits my lifestyle by making me feel more embodied and in tune with the world around me. I've been consuming it for years. I often use ceremonial-grade cacao in full moon ceremonies to help facilitate the opening of my mind, body and heart.

If you would like to add raw cacao to your diet, start small and build up gradually. Sweeten or flavour it with natural sweeteners such as stevia, monk fruit, raw honey or rice malt syrup. Cacao can be used to make homemade chocolate or chocolate sauce to pour over dairy-free ice cream or pancakes. You can also add it to your smoothies or morning oats.

CAFFEINE

Coffee rocks my goddamn socks. I love coffee, and I believe it's a beautiful gift that can be included in a healthy lifestyle, if it is used in the right way and doesn't have any negative side effects on your health. Coffee is high in antioxidants and can be a great natural way to get your bowels moving in the morning. Here are some healthy caffeine habits.

- Hydrate before you caffeinate.
- If your body doesn't respond well to dairy, try swapping to black coffee or lattes made with plant-based milk.
- If you lack energy, don't reach for caffeine. It can adversely affect your adrenal glands. These glands produce important hormones such as cortisol, which helps your body regulate stress.
- Avoid drinking coffee after midday, to ensure it's out of your system before bed. Caffeine from coffee or black tea can affect your sleep up to 6 hours after consumption
- Have a break from caffeine for a week now and again.

- Buy high-quality coffee (organic if possible). Coffee is one of the most sprayed crops in the world. By buying organic coffee, you can reduce your intake of toxins as well as support the environment and better farming practices.

ALCOHOL

I am here to support you to embrace a positive relationship with drinking alcohol. I drank heavily as a teen. Weekends were spent getting wasted, followed by Sunday brunch blissing out on a big bag of hot chippies from the takeaway shop across the road.

The days of being a crazy teenager were quite fun … but the next day, getting wasted left me feeling terrible. Once I moved into adulthood, I began to notice how alcohol adversely affects many people in our society.

I stopped drinking at age 19. Once in a blue moon, I will have a few drinks (tequila soda or red wine) with family or friends, but it's just not for me. I don't like the way it alters my perception, how it makes me feel, and how it upsets my stomach. Personally, I always have *loads* more fun when I am out with my friends and not drinking.

There is nothing wrong with having a few drinks, as long as it doesn't negatively impact your health. If you find yourself drinking alone, binge drinking, turning to alcohol to suppress uncomfortable feelings or you just don't like the way alcohol makes your mind and body feel, this may be a great time to reassess your relationship with alcohol and rewrite your story.

YOU DON'T NEED ALCOHOL TO HAVE FUN!

Last night, I had a brilliant night out with my girlfriends. We danced like crazy till 11 pm and went to bed at midnight. I had loads of fun, had stacks of high-vibing energy (thanks to the practices in this book) and had a beautiful evening *sober*. If you don't have a healthy relationship with alcohol and want to stop drinking it, please remember that you don't have to miss out on dinners, parties or music festivals. You can still have a social life if you don't drink alcohol. I love raving at music festivals with my hydration backpack full of water.

IT'S OKAY TO SAY NO

Your real friends or social group will not judge you for not having a drink. If they do, then maybe they aren't the right community to support you on your journey. I have spoken to many friends about this topic and each person has said how much respect and gratitude they have for a friend who chooses not to drink alcohol, whether it's for a weekend, a few weeks or a longer duration of time.

HEALTHY DRINKING HABITS

Healthy drinking habits are ways of celebrating that enhance your life and don't leave you feeling regretful or experiencing unpleasant health effects. To me, healthy drinking habits are about honouring your body's needs and choosing to drink for the right reasons. Here are some of my healthy tips on drinking alcohol.

- Skip pre-mixed drinks containing sugar.
- Stick to high-quality spirits (preferably clear) with soda water and fresh lemon or lime.
- Avoid mixing different liquors.
- Hydrate! Drink a glass of water between your drinks.
- Refuel your body with high-quality nutrition the next day. Opt for greens and healthy fats, and fulfil any salt cravings with a homemade savoury meal. Salt helps to rehydrate the body from the dehydrating effects of alcohol. Nutritious breakfast choices after a night out include a green smoothie with avocado toast, fresh fruit or scrambled eggs and veggies.

- Try and get some sunshine and movement the next day. Walking or swimming will do wonders for your body and mind after a night out.

You get to decide what makes you feel good and what doesn't. Try not to let other people's opinions cloud your judgement. This is *your* life and it's time to start living the one you desire. As you work through the practices and chapters in this book, you will have more confidence to stand up for your beliefs and values. If you're ready to say 'no' to drinking alcohol, you've got this, and I've got you too.

In this book we are creating your unique superhero toolkit, so choose the equipment you want to carry and let go of the rest.

To love oneself is the icing on the cake of life — without it things are pretty bland

It's Not Just About *What* You Eat

Food is a gift to savour, appreciate and cultivate deep gratitude for. When we talk about food and eating, it's not just about *what* you're eating, it's also about *how* you're eating.

FOOD FACT

Different foods have different rates at which they digest. For example, fruit eaten on its own can be in and out of the stomach in 20 to 40 minutes (hence why it is a great pre-workout snack). Grains can take around 90 minutes to move through the digestive tract and proteins 120 minutes plus! However, it doesn't end there. There are four main phases of digestion and, according to research by Dian Dooley, it can take about 24–72 hours for most people to completely digest and eliminate food. In the study, it took around 3 days for a processed hamburger to digest due to the high fat content (holy crap, I know!). Understanding the rate in which particular foods digest can help you to make better dietary choices. If you need energy in the morning to do a workout, opt for lighter, easy-digesting foods.

Fruit craves rapid digestion, so if you are trying to digest a lunch full of carbs, proteins and healthy fats and grab an after-meal snack of fruit, the fruit can sit on the top wanting to digest, but is stuck in the traffic line. The sugars in the fruit can then begin to ferment, causing belly troubles such as bloating or gurgling. Understanding this process can help you recognise if you may need to reorder the foods you eat. If you struggle with belly troubles, a little fruit in your smoothies is usually fine, as blending fast-tracks the digestive process and maintains the fruit's fibre.

EAT A BALANCE OF MACRONUTRIENTS

Macronutrients are proteins, carbohydrates and fats. Eating meals with a balance of macros will help to stabilise your mood, appetite and blood-sugar levels. One of the first macros we look at to stabilise blood sugars is carbohydrates. Carbs are metabolised quickly, providing a rapid source of energy. But when eaten on their own, they can leave us craving more carbs within a few hours, so it's helpful to add healthy fats or protein to your carb meals, as this will balance your hunger hormones, mood and energy. For example, toast (carbohydrate) with a spread (carbohydrate) for breakfast can leave you looking for another quick energy hit (and blood-sugar spike). To bring a belly of contentment, add avocado, veggies or eggs to your toast. Love oatmeal? Add a scoop of plant-based protein powder.

TIPS TO HELP MINIMISE TUMMY TROUBLE

- Take three deep belly breaths (see page 37) before each meal to calm your nervous system. You might also choose to meditate before and after eating.
- Be mindful of your posture while eating. Do your best to sit up straight and not hunch over.

- Space out your meals and snacks so that your food can properly digest.
- Avoid eating fruit with, or directly after, meals.
- To help digestion, lightly steam or cook your vegetables and massage raw leafy greens in salt, olive oil or acids such as lemon juice or apple cider vinegar, to help break down the tough fibrous leaves.
- Apple cider vinegar (ACV) can help support digestion. Take ACV in water with or just after food to support hydrochloric acid (stomach acid) production, which is used to break down foods. I love to drink 1 tablespoon of ACV in a glass of water early in the morning. Check with your health professional first to see if ACV is suitable for you.
- Most of us know about probiotics, which contain live forms of bacteria and yeast that are great for gut health (found in things like yoghurt, kimchi and pickles), but prebiotics are just as important, so make sure to include both in your diet. Prebiotics are found in foods such as green bananas, apple, garlic, onion and sweet potatoes.
- Try to drink water mindfully to avoid swallowing excess air.
- Avoid consuming excessive amounts of bubbly drinks. Even soda water can result in extra bubbles in the belly that may cause discomfort.

GENERAL HEALTHY HACKS

- Craving sweets after dinner? Eat a spoonful of a healthy source of fat first, such as coconut oil or nut butter. Or make some homemade chocolate or hot chocolate using raw cacao or cacao powder.
- At mealtimes, load up on brassica veggies, such as broccoli, cauliflower, cabbage and brussels sprouts. These veggies are high in antioxidants, vitamins and minerals.

- Coconut oil 'pulling' is great for the health of teeth and gums, as it reduces the amount of harmful bacterial in your mouth. Take 1 tablespoon of liquid coconut oil, put it in your mouth, swish it around for 15–20 minutes and then spit it out.
- Drink veggie juices for glowing skin.
- Prioritise magnesium. Some magnesium-rich foods are spinach, lima beans, brown rice, dark chocolate (at least 70 per cent cocoa) or cacao, and pumpkin seeds.
- Raw garlic has antibacterial properties. I like to use it in salad dressings and sometimes I swallow it whole. Make sure to take into account your individual health circumstances, as there are some conditions such as IBS (irritable bowel syndrome) that don't tolerate garlic.

EATING RHYTHM

This refers to the timing of your meals. Not having a regular eating rhythm can create habits such as skipping breakfast and lunch, resulting in undesired snacking or bingeing in the evenings. Creating harmony in your eating rhythm means not skipping meals. In Ayurvedic medicine (the sister science of yoga), it is suggested that the largest meal of the day should be eaten when the sun is at its highest point in the sky. This is at midday and is when the digestive system is said to be firing most efficiently. Your body's needs are individual but, as I learned in the psychology of eating, if you are indulging at night, then make it a priority to eat good food throughout the day.

Studies show that a balanced eating rhythm, aka eating meals at the same time each day, can help balance the metabolism, leading to a greater chance of success in goals such as weight loss. So, if you are struggling with weight and eating a healthy diet, it might be a good opportunity to look at your eating rhythm and macronutrient balance. Make sure you are getting a good balance of healthy carbs, proteins and healthy fats, avoiding carb-only meals and not skipping meals. If you're always reaching for snacks, try introducing more healthy fats to your diet, such as avocado, hummus, tahini and most nuts.

SLOW DOWN

Do you eat meals while your attention is on another task? Let me tell you what happens when we eat this way. We finish our meal and the belly is satisfied, but all the other senses of the body miss out on the experience of eating, which can leave a residual 'hunger'-like feeling. This feeling isn't one of physical hunger, but a craving for the pleasurable, sensual experience of food. The missed presence, sights and smells can send us once again back to the cupboard or fridge to look for more food.

When we eat fast, the body can go into a stress response, affecting cortisol levels. Studies show that cortisol can have a negative impact on our digestion, and has an increased link to obesity and fat storage. The great news? You can become a slow, sexy, embodied eater.

When I think about what is sexy, being slow and embodied arises in my mind. Slowing down in life and with eating isn't easy, but it is beautiful. Out of all the healing practices I implemented on my food journey, slowing down and eating in a relaxed state was at the forefront of my transformation. I experienced a considerable decrease in gastric distress and bloating. Symptoms I had spent a fortune trying to fix with supplements and trips to the naturopath and nutritionist began to disappear.

Bringing awareness to your food and eating habits requires you to ask these questions: *Are you a fast or slow eater? Do you eat on the run or while multitasking with television, emails or scrolling on your phone? Do you shovel food in without thinking as you make lunch or dinner?* If you are a fast eater, becoming a slow eater will require work. Remember to commit to the process and remind yourself to breathe and *slow down.*

Slow Eating

Slowing down and relaxing with food requires some simple actions.

1. Before eating, take 10 deep breaths with your feet centred on the ground.

2. Switch off the television and your phone. Don't eat on the run. Be present and seated at mealtimes.

3. Make time for meals, even if it's only 10–15 minutes.

4. Don't scoff your food. Slow down. Make sure you're belly breathing (see page 37) while you eat. Chew loads more times than you think you should.

DROP THE GUILT

There will be times when you will eat fast foods or indulge in a meal you typically don't eat. In these moments, don't beat yourself up, as this can cause stress and feelings of unworthiness. Negative thoughts can cause the body more damage than food itself. Instead, do your best to create an internal food dialogue of compassion and understanding. Challenge negative thoughts and welcome more positive alternatives. For example, if you have the thought, *I can't believe I ate all of that,* a more compassionate alternative would be, *Sometimes it's okay to eat what I feel like, I was doing my best.*

Enjoy What You Eat

You cannot expect to thrive if you don't have adequate food nourishment. And the way you eat directly impacts your overall wellbeing. Getting the love and enjoyment your body needs from food is essential.

Nourishment (which I liken to enjoyment in what you eat) will relax your body, helping you to feel calm and content. Humans thrive on food enjoyment; without pleasure from food, the body can become tight and stressed. Remember the negative impacts we learned about stress? This response can lead to digestive shutdown, nutrient secretion and fat storage. Therefore, often when we are stuck and cannot shift or lose weight, we have lost *pleasure*.

No pleasure in the diet can be seen in meal plans that offer no flexibility. Many people who undergo strict diets during competitions such as bodybuilding or high-level sports face the negative effects of removing nourishment, which can lead to poor mental health or unwanted habits.

Removing nourishment from your life affects your overall wellbeing. Imagine you are a big clear body of water made up of lots of flowing streams. These streams are the different pillars of your health and lifestyle, such as diet, relationships, movement, hobbies, etc. If one of the streams gets dirty, it will affect the big body of water, aka you. Removing pleasure from one fundamental aspect of your lifestyle will have an impact on the other parts of your health.

Pleasure from food is *healing*. Enjoyment in your diet will help you to relax and feel more at ease in life. I felt my world transform from this practice. Can you look for places to receive more love in your diet? Enjoy the foods you eat! This means that if you have a strong craving to eat chocolate, then eat a small amount − and enjoy it. If you adore going out for your favourite pasta, then you can keep this as a part of your nourishing food lifestyle. Your mindset, thoughts and intentions should be connected with nourishment. *Eat for pleasure. Love your food and feel good about having it.*

Nourish Yourself

- Have gratitude for your food.

- Mindfully eat and drink.

- Listen to and honour your body's cravings.

- Cook and prepare meals that you love.

- Eat or share mealtimes with loved ones, family or friends.

- Buy high-quality ingredients if you can, and don't restrict your food choices due to feelings of unworthiness.

If you are stuck in rules of eating the same bland or repetitive foods every day, begin to challenge these rules. Include variety in your diet and eat more foods that you enjoy. Challenging these habits may not be easy at first, but it will get easier. I know this because I was there for years. I lost nourishment and, as a result, other parts of my world became dull.

INTUITIVE EATING

Intuitive eating is essentially listening to your body and eating in accordance with its needs, wants and desires, while still remaining focused on general good nutrition and prioritising real food. This means asking questions before you eat, such as: *What do I feel like eating today? What food desires does my body have?*

Intuitive eating can bring food freedom. When I first started to practise intuitive eating, I was like, *Wait, maybe my body doesn't want the same damn thing for breakfast every day. Maybe it has needs that fluctuate like my hormones, emotions and feelings.* I became inquisitive. These days, after a few years of letting my intuition be my guide to food, most of my meals are different.

Eating intuitively is about being in flow and enjoying the changing nature of the body's cravings. It's about relaxing and cultivating ease around food. Here is the lowdown on intuitive eating.

Stock Up – Having a fridge and pantry full of different foods is an excellent start for intuitive eating. Options provide you with a chance to think about what you feel like before you eat and to prepare the meal accordingly. I recommend contemplating a variety of meals and doing a weekly shop so that you are prepared.

Ponder – A short time before you eat your meal, check in with your body. Ask your body what it wants and listen to its desires. Sweet? Savoury? Grounding? Light? Grounding foods are heavier and warming foods such as those high in proteins and fats, rich flavours, and nuts, root vegetables, lentils and beans. Examples of lighter foods are fruits, salads, rice paper rolls, raw veggies and stir-fries. Tune in to your body and listen to what foods it's telling you it's craving.

Keep a Food Diary – Keeping a food diary is a great way to gain clarity on how certain foods make you feel. For a few weeks, write about your meals and the way you feel throughout the day. This practice should give you some great information on the foods that make you feel good and the foods that don't. You don't need to do this long term. It's just a simple tool to help you find out what makes you feel good. Things that you may wish to jot down in your food journal include topics such as:

- how you feel before and after you eat
- what you eat
- how fast you eat
- energy levels
- mental focus
- digestion
- mood
- hunger.

Remember: You are individual and the way you eat should be unique. If your body thrives on six small meals a day, great! If you only eat three meals each day, that's okay too! Rather than looking at what others do, just do you.

A POSITIVE FOOD RELATIONSHIP

A positive food relationship is one that is loving and free. The feelings that are essential to cultivate a positive relationship with food are compassion, non-judgement and understanding. Developing a loving and free relationship with food means there are *no rules about what you can and can't eat.* In a balanced diet, this means you can have your cake and eat it too. There is no fear needed.

Try this

A POSITIVE FOOD MANTRA

Create a positive food mantra or affirmation. Write it down and repeat it to yourself daily or before meals. This exercise can help to rewire your relationship with food.

If you have a challenging relationship with food, it's often not food that's the issue; it can go much deeper. Ask questions and start to uncover the layers that are hiding under your uncomfortable relationship with food. *What is at the core of your feelings simmering underneath the surface? What part of your wellbeing do you truly need to focus on?* Often the core of food negativity can stem from feelings of unworthiness, poor body image or lack of self-love. It's important to remember that food is not the enemy.

Wherever you are in your relationship with food, I encourage you to try and embrace your journey. Try to be okay with your past and accept where you are now, no matter what it looks like. Everything up until this point has been an essential part of your growth and journey towards a life of *food freedom*.

A POSITIVE FOOD LIFESTYLE

Our choices have an impact on the world around us. Adopting a positive food lifestyle means being a conscious consumer. The world is our sanctuary so we need to take care of it. You can help the economy and planet by making some simple lifestyle choices such as: shopping local, visiting farmers' markets over supermarkets, reducing waste, recycling jars and refilling your pantry at the bulk store, only buying what you need, saying no to plastic bags and carrying a reusable straw and cutlery when eating out.

Healing from Disordered Eating

The most profound wisdom I gained from studying the psychology of eating, and through recovering from an eating disorder is that struggles with eating are *not about the food*. Unwanted eating habits are often an indication that something else is out of balance. Marc David, the founder of the Institute for the Psychology of Eating, refers to these habits as 'divine symptoms' that don't exist to cause harm but to offer an opportunity to transform. Yes, everything is connected.

When healing disordered eating habits, the first step is about understanding that our challenges or 'symptoms' are requesting our attention on a deeper level. To move past the symptoms, we once again need to be curious and ask questions about the disequilibrium (imbalance) we're experiencing, and find out what it may be trying to teach us.

When we experience unwanted eating habits and focus on the symptom itself, we are fixating on the surface, which is not the root of the cause. To positively grow and transform our relationship with food, we need to dig deeper.

When you open your mind and heart to a more curious and inquisitive way of being, you will see how every obstacle you face in life can be viewed as a doorway for transformation – an opportunity to grow and evolve. Each time we choose to use non-judgement and loving curiosity, we become more embodied. As you feel more open and relaxed, you may notice that walls that were blocking your path begin to dissolve. In this state of ease, contentment and clarity can arise. This process allows you to move out of your mind and into your heart.

A difficult relationship with food can be a way to express a difficult relationship with yourself. A revelation in my eating disorder recovery unfolded when I began to understand the way my food habits were an expression of my confusion and difficulties in life. I began to look for the correlation. A change in my perspective helped me to understand the way my eating disorder went beyond food and was connected to my emotions. As I began to understand myself more, I felt my grip on food and my body loosen. My recovery showed me that our inner world affects our outer world, and the way we relate to food.

TRANSFORMATIONAL HEALING

I like to view unwanted habits as *portholes to transformation*. For true healing to occur, the first step is to look beneath the surface of the symptom. Your hunger isn't just physical. Emotional and spiritual hunger also exist. For example, the symptom of 'restrictive eating' could be due to trapped emotional trauma. The way to heal and move forward may be to visit a psychologist for therapy and try healing practices such as meditation and journalling.

You can practise mindfulness and start to ask questions about your cravings that manifest as hunger (physically, emotionally and spiritually). For example, are you eating chips after work as a form of stress relief? Is there a healthier alternative you could implement instead? Maybe what you are actually craving is breathwork, a walk in nature or some yoga. You may begin to see that there is more than one form of hunger.

Through mindfulness, I can cultivate awareness of when my food cravings are coming from an emotional place. Awareness is what allows you to consciously honour your body's cravings. For example, I might make the decision to sit down and enjoy a sweet hot chocolate to create feelings of love. It's a positive action because I am being conscious. I am allowing the hot chocolate to fill me with love and nourishment, and I am present.

Before you eat, check in with how you feel: *Am I feeling anxious, sad or stressed right now? Am I hungry, or is my body craving nourishment from something else?* The answers to these questions can help you decide consciously what action to take.

If you are struggling with unwanted behaviours such as a food addiction, binge eating, overeating or food obsessions, support is available and it is possible to move past your symptoms. Consulting a qualified health professional can be an important starting point.

In all your discovery work, I encourage you to treat yourself with kindness, care and understanding. Being a human is both complex and beautiful. Keep showing up and doing the work. Your intention, dedication and efforts won't go unnoticed. And remember, always ask for help if and when you need it.

Part 4

VALUE YOURSELF

The Self-Love Club

Welcome to the Self-love Club! Self-love means having compassion and understanding for ourselves, embracing our power and believing in our dreams and heart's desires. Self-love means becoming a friend to ourselves, prioritising a mindset of loving kindness and being dedicated to our health and happiness.

BE INSPIRED BY OTHERS

During a quick bathroom stop at the Splendour in the Grass music festival, I came across a young woman with long dark hair and alluring confidence. As I was washing my hands, she asked whether I was the girl from *Puberty Blues* (this is the line I get most often). We struck up a conversation about the show.

I asked who she was with at the festival. She told me that she was from Perth and in town on her own. Her friends promised they would buy tickets to the festival when she purchased hers, but none went through with their promise. Her boyfriend also broke up with her a few days prior, and here she was, on her own. I was amazed and inspired by her courage. I scooped her arm in mine and said, 'Honey, you're coming with me. Let's tango.'

She was the definition of a warrior. Not blaming her misfortune on the universe and not feeling sorry for herself for the series of unfortunate events that took place before her 4-hour red-eye flight to an Airbnb in Ocean Shores. She showed up. Her very presence exuded that she wore her heart on her sleeve, was open to experiences and said, 'World, I'm here. I am in charge of my life, and I'm going to have a fucking great weekend without anyone else.'

This is just one example of being a warrior. This woman showed me the power of having high self-worth and independence. Her dedication to her happiness and worth allowed her to live the life she chooses – one that isn't dictated by events, people or experiences outside of her control.

Self-love is like the sun to the earth. Without it, we cannot flourish. It's an epic life necessity. Nothing will make you more beautiful than learning to love yourself. However, self-love can look different for all

How can I be kinder to myself today?

of us, and you might like to journal about what it means to you. Here are some different ways to describe self-love.

- Deep acceptance.
- Remembering to love oneself in the present moment.
- Being okay and at peace with all that you are.
- Giving to others.
- Doing things you enjoy.

Self-love is a journey. It calls for conscious daily action, which involves prioritising mindfulness and self-love habits. Following are my favourite positive psychology tips for creating a mindset of self-love.

AWARENESS

Awareness is simply noticing the way we think, act and feel towards ourselves and others. Start to take note and shine a light on what arises internally for you in different situations.

As we practise awareness, the key is to be non-judgemental. For this practice, I personally like to set my intention to one of 'intrigue', by which I mean observing without judgement. If you notice that your mind chatter is quite toxic in certain situations, do *not* beat yourself up about it. Simply try to change your internal dialogue to one of compassion and understanding.

As you practise awareness, take note of places where you need to sprinkle some magic self-love dust. Are negative thoughts present? Does your mind chatter or your beliefs limit the way you feel? Maybe you catch sight of your own reflection and pick on yourself? Are there moments when you want to do something or take action, but you are hindered by feelings of fear or unworthiness? Perhaps write down any thoughts that arise in your journal. If you notice you feel negativity towards yourself after work, put some sticky notes in your car saying nice things about you, that you'll see when you get in.

CREATE AN INVENTORY OF YOUR THOUGHTS

Begin to create an inventory of your thoughts in relation to your sense of self-worth. You may notice that some negative thoughts are 'repeat offenders', for example: *You're not good at that, so don't even try it.* When you discover these repeat offenders, it might be useful to try to use humour to combat them. I catch mine and say, *Dude, you're old. You can't limit my greatness!* After using this practice, I know my repeat offenders well. They often like to get me in times of stress. I tell them politely that they are not true and I say to myself, *You've got this.*

It's helpful to try and uncover the triggers of your negative thoughts. For example, some may always arise when you're using social media or with a particular person. Uncovering these triggers can give you an opportunity (where possible) to remove these influences. Here are some questions to contemplate in your journal.

- What are your repeat offenders (recurring negative thoughts)?
- Can you uncover the trigger(s) to any negative thoughts?
- Can you create some positive substitutes for these negative thoughts?
- How can you be kinder to yourself today?

DEVELOP A BALANCED PERSPECTIVE

Once you practise consciously being aware of your thoughts and self-talk, you create the space to catch any negative thoughts when they arise and try and view them with a more balanced perspective. If you notice an unhelpful thought popping into your mind, pause and choose to transform it into something more balanced or positive by asking yourself, *What is a kinder, more logical thought?* It's all about practice and the more times you can catch a negative thought and transform it into something else more loving or balanced, the more resilient your mind will become.

RADICAL ACCEPTANCE

One of the key pillars of self-love is acceptance. 'Radical acceptance' is the ability to accept our realities completely, instead of fighting them. It's about finding peace with where we are right now. Radical acceptance does not take away from growth and becoming a better version of ourself. Instead, it's about feeling enough in who we are and where we are today, and it can allow us to build and evolve in a way that is rooted in love.

So, how do you build radical acceptance? By remembering that you are not your thoughts – they are constructs of your mind – and by practising healthy habits, caring for your heart and developing an internal dialogue of respect and compassion. A lot of the things we discuss in this book are tools for cultivating self-acceptance.

LOOK AT POSITIVE ROLE MODELS

When I am feeling overwhelmed or facing a difficult experience that causes my thoughts to spiral, I create a list of attributes I see in others that I appreciate or want to cultivate. I spend time looking at positive role models and reflecting on the things I love about them. I then might jot them down in my journal.

Try this

LOOK FOR THE LIGHT IN OTHERS

Take note and look for the good, or the light, in people you meet. Can you shine that light you see in others back onto yourself? If you look carefully, you might find places inside you where these good qualities are hiding. Work on highlighting these and bringing them to the surface.

I ♡ you
I respect you
I accept you
I am.

SELF-LOVE BOOSTERS

To boost self-love, I always make time for self-care and connecting with nature. These practices help me to clear my mind and feel grounded and in alignment. Whenever I'm in a negative body funk, I love to practise earthing or dance. What are your favourite self-care practices? Write them down in your journal and carve out time for these sacred practices in your everyday life.

REMOVE NEGATIVE INFLUENCES

You have a choice about who you follow on social media, what magazines and resources you read and the people you surround yourself with. The self-love and awareness exercises in this part of the book can help to uncover the places, people and situations that trigger negative thoughts for you. Try and remove these negative influences, unfollow social accounts that make you feel like shit, and become inquisitive about the environments or people in your life that cause you stress.

If you can't remove certain negative influences, I find it helpful to acknowledge and feel everything the experience brings up, and then breathe deep into my belly (see page 37) to bring calmness and clarity. Once I've honoured my feelings, I let them flow out and focus on choosing an empowering way to move forward. This is often as simple as having compassion.

Affirmations and Mantras

Affirmations

An affirmation involves repeating a series of words or phrases for emotional support, encouragement or to assist with change. Affirmations can help us to highlight our more positive attributes and they're a potent self-love tool.

I create different affirmations depending on my needs. An affirmation is unique to *your* needs. It may be short or long. You don't need to memorise it. You can read it out of your journal or phone. It can be repeated every week, every day or multiple times a day – find your sweet spot.

Your personal affirmation should be based on words of encouragement or the personal strengths and qualities you have or want to strengthen. I like to focus on making them motivational. Where people often go wrong with affirmations is when they aim too high too soon. Focus on meeting yourself one step higher than where you are now, then working your way up.

One of my recent affirmations was: *I believe in myself. I am grounded and I trust in my work.* I also benefited from an affirmation practice when working on my relationship with food and healing my digestion. My affirmation was: *I can have a healthy relationship with food. My digestion is strong.*

If you are really struggling with self-love, maybe your first affirmation is: *I accept myself.* As your self-love strengthens, you may be able to alter your affirmation to: *I love myself.*

Mantras

Mantra is a Sanskrit word that originated from an ancient Vedic tradition. You may be familiar with one yogic mantra in particular – 'Om' – as it is often used in yoga classes. Mantras involve a word or phrase that you repeat, and are designed to help you stay present by focusing the mind. You can repeat a mantra in your mind or say it out loud.

I find it beneficial to create my own mantras and find this tool useful when my mind is spiralling and I need to bring it back to centre. Reciting a mantra saved my declining mental state once when I found myself in a difficult circumstance. Simply repeating my mantra for the 30 minutes it took me to get home enabled me to stay focused so that I didn't panic. I find mantras work best when the phrase is short, sweet and potent. You can create one that suits your needs and change it whenever you like.

You can also meditate with your mantra. I do this when I'm working on opening my heart, improving self-love or calling in creativity. Some of my past mantras have been:

Let go

*

I've got this

*

Surrender

*

I am enough

REMEMBER YOU'RE A WARRIOR

Cultivating a strong sense of self-love will positively transform your world. Negative thought patterns and self-doubt have a more considerable impact than we might realise. In Part 1 we learned that nothing positive comes from shaming others, so why do we feel the need to do it to ourselves? Telling yourself that you are not enough can fill you with negative energy and lead you to believe that these thoughts are true … but there is a way out! The first step is to realise that *you* have the power. Speak to yourself as you would speak to somebody you love, or if that is initially too hard, then start with someone you respect. Encourage yourself throughout this self-love journey.

I know you are a warrior. I know that you are aware that life is a beautiful dance and you want to experience its depths in a positive, balanced way. Keep doing the work and be the person who walks into a room with love, respect and acceptance for who they are. Confidence is sexy. When I witness somebody embracing exactly who they are, I am drawn to them, as they radiate an aura that is confident, warm and empowered.

At times, the healing and improvement process can feel slow, but just remember that you have the power.

Self-Care

S elf-care is an act done deliberately to take care of your mental, physical and spiritual wellbeing. Self-care can improve your mood, reduce anxiety, relieve stress, boost your energy and help you to make positive decisions. The results of a US 2018 questionnaire completed by more than 850 medical students showed that individuals who used self-care practices reported a decrease in their perceived stress and an increase in quality of life. Some days, when I'm feeling a little blue, I'll jump into the shower with a jar of coconut oil and massage my body as an act of self-care. Other days, my self-care might be going to a workout class or having a relaxing bath with fragrant essential oils.

Self-care involves tangible exercises or habits that strengthen our self-worth and self-love. Each time we choose to prioritise caring for ourselves, we are creating a strong foundation to support us in the world each day. I view self-care as a way to keep myself on track, or to fill myself back up when I'm feeling depleted. We may do things for ourselves every day, but it's the act of doing them mindfully and in a nurturing way that makes them an act of self-care. It's beneficial to set a self-care intention for your chosen practice(s).

The beauty of creating your epic life is that there are *no* rules. I don't want you to feel like self-care or any healthy habit has to involve lengthy acts in your already busy life. Self-care simply means acts of nourishment that are done on a regular basis out of respect and love. Try to think of self-care like a soul recharge.

Take note of things that interest you and write them down. You may wish to put a 'self-care' reminder somewhere you will see it, such as on your fridge or bedroom wall. I enjoy dedicating one day of the week ('self-care Sunday') to my practices.

If you don't know where to start with self-care, try a few different things to see what works and what doesn't. Your self-care might involve long baths and beauty services, or it may involve playing guitar, or even just having healthy boundaries and saying no to social events when you need downtime. Some other ideas involve getting a massage, reading a book, meditating, yoga, journalling, going to a dance class, spending time in nature, baking or creating art.

SELF-CARE LIST

Ask yourself these questions in your journal to create an individual self-care list.

- What fills me back up if I feel depleted?
- What makes my mind and body feel good?
- What makes me happy?
- What things do I love to do?

SOMETIMES WE NEED REMINDING

It was a peaceful Saturday afternoon, but I was feeling off-balance. My mind felt like it had miswired cables. I ventured to the beach for a run to try to clear my head. Post-run, during my scrambled thoughts, I remembered a lovely new friend that I'd recently met who lived down the street. I sent her a text: 'I'm hanging in my van by the sea if you're free for a chat'. Within a minute, I had a reply: 'I'm just finishing some yoga by the lake. I'll ride my bike to you before my swim.'

There she was. Amelia (let's call her that) radiated everything I wish to encompass in this book: naturalness, simplicity and love. She was exactly the reminder I needed at this time – a friend and woman relishing in the simple pleasures of a wholesome life. Her grounding energy swept me up and I felt like myself again.

In our brief afternoon chat, she taught me more about myself and my mission than I could have ever wished for. Before our chat, my mind was wired hot. I was over-worked, over-stimulated and caught up in all the big stresses of life. I didn't feel good. Amelia brought me back down to earth and reminded me of the importance of thinking small, self-care and connecting with the person that I was at heart. Her Saturday evening plans were yoga by the lake followed by a swim in the ocean, salt bath and face mask. Just her presence exuded harmony. She put my life back into perspective. All my big worries of the world seemed to evaporate, and I was able to see what was really important: balance, self-love and honouring my feminine self. I'd lost my Yin and it was time to stop burning the candle at both ends.

I drove home, turned off the lights, lit some candles and embraced self-care. After surrendering to my nourishing practices, everything made sense and I realised that I needed love. The true essence of this feeling comes from the heart by cultivating deep compassion and warmth towards yourself. I had let myself get off-track. I lost my sense of self-care and self-love and I felt like downright shit. Amelia filled my heart and reminded me that it's about the simple acts, and I want to remind you of this too.

Self-Worth

Self-worth is your value of yourself. I believe it is grown by cultivating respect for yourself – the kind of respect you have for loved ones and people you admire. Respecting myself means honouring my feelings, understanding that I am worthy of speaking up in times of need, looking after myself when I feel run down and encouraging myself to move towards my goals when I am not living up to my potential. Healthy habits can help to develop self-worth. For example, journalling and self-enquiry can lead to a greater understanding of yourself, which then can help you to recognise what self-worth means to you.

I want to share with you three different stories about self-worth.

1. Years ago, I made the conscious choice to let go of drinking alcohol. I have nothing against drinking in a balanced way, it's just not for me. Time and time again when I'm out, I will get passed a drink, asked to drink or sometimes told to, 'Just have a drink'. My

strong foundation of self-worth allows me to sit in my power and politely decline any offers. I never feel embarrassed or pressured, or second-guess my decision not to drink. My decisions are active choices based on my values and beliefs.

2. I was at a dance party with my friends and family. The crowd was huge. Everyone was feeling liberated and having a blast. Sparkles were shimmering, love-heart sunnies were on, shirts were off and dance moves were being dropped all around. It was full of fun, uplifting energy (my mum was even on her husband's shoulders!). A young man was standing next to me and I overheard him loudly declare something rude about one of my family members. My self-worth kicked in and I tapped the guy on the shoulder and said: 'Excuse me, I just heard what you said about my family member. It was not a nice comment and it made me feel uncomfortable. We are all having a great time and it would be nice if you kept your harsh words to yourself.' He was taken aback. My self-worth gave me the confidence to express how I felt in the situation. You have a right to politely assert yourself at any time and in any place. By having clarity on my personal values, I know what behaviour I tolerate and what I don't. This story demonstrates the power of living by your values. Seeking clarity on what you value will support your sense of self-worth.

After leaving a long-term relationship, I now spend a lot of time diving into self-development, which has resulted in time out from the dating world. But thanks to some friends, I still get juicy insight into how dating games can play out via apps such as Bumble and Tinder. The same stories kept surfacing. I was surprised to hear how many young people feel obliged to sleep with someone after a night out, a date or a few dates. In my third story I will explain how your sense of self-worth can influence your romantic decisions.

3. Over the past few years, I have experimented with meeting new guys via dating apps. With myself back in the dating grind and with a strong sense of self-worth, I found myself getting to know an amazing guy, but I realised that I just wasn't ready to have sex with him. So I told him: 'I adore you and I love making out with you, but I'm not ready to have sex with you at the moment. I want to wait.' Before doing this work on myself, I don't think I would have had the courage to say this. I expressed how I felt and he respected my honesty. We continued to date for months.

Another experience played out a little differently. I started chatting to a new guy from a dating app. The first date was quite lovely, but within an hour he asked me to sleep over. I declined politely, as I really didn't know this guy. We then arranged another date. I was all dressed up and ready to go but then he cancelled our dinner and show plans and asked to get a late drink instead. My red flags started waving, but I gave him the benefit of the doubt. We met up, and his whole persona was entirely different from our initial date. I tried my best to brush off the awkward vibe, wondering if he was just nervous. He made a few attempts to get me to drink, next came an unexpected hand up my leg and then I decided it was time to go home. He insisted on following me outside to my car, attempting again to try and get intimate with me, followed by an offer to go to his campervan. I replied, 'No thanks, I am heading home.' He was super withdrawn and somewhat shocked when he realised I was actually leaving. After that night, he never messaged me again.

Your sexual body is precious property, and you *do not* have to have intercourse of any kind with someone if you are not ready. On the other hand, remember that it's okay to have sex with someone whenever you want, as long as it's on *both your* terms. It's important to build self-worth so that you can take action *before* events happen, which may leave you with unwanted feelings, such as regret or feeling like a victim. My self-worth helps me to feel empowered, rather than disempowered, after particular events if I handle them the way I want. This is why we need to prioritise building self-worth. A strong core will enable you to express your desires confidently in any situation.

HOW CAN YOU BUILD SELF-WORTH?

Practising self-care and radical acceptance, defining your boundaries and values as well as working with your mind are all powerful ways to build your self-worth.

Spend time defining your boundaries by asking: *What is acceptable in my world, and what is unacceptable?* Knowing what aligns with your values can help you to stick up for yourself in times of need. One of my values is to always speak my truth. Having self-worth gives me the ability to make the right decisions in the moment and to stand up for what I believe in.

Creating boundaries and speaking up for yourself are some of the most powerful actions you can take. I always like to ponder what the worst thing that could happen is, and it's never as bad as the thought of not speaking truthfully. For example, if you choose not to sleep with someone and they don't call you again, I believe this is a blessing in disguise. The right person will respect your choices – but remember to express your feelings to them in a kind way.

If your self-worth is low at the moment, that is okay. Respect the journey and honour where you are right now. Self-worth is like a muscle – it will strengthen the more you use it.

Don't forget that the body is a system, and everything we work on in this book will support you in strengthening your epic life qualities such as strong self-worth and self-love.

Change and Self-Discovery

One of my friends recently came out of a long-term relationship. We sat on my bedroom floor for hours, chatting about our lives. 'I just feel like I wasted so much time and lost myself,' he said. I replied, 'Sometimes, I think that the feeling of losing yourself is a blessing, because you get to discover more of who you are.'

Every life experience you have can be perceived as either positive or negative, depending on your outlook. But if you embrace a growth mindset, each setback or mistake can be seen as a valuable lesson. Feeling like you have lost yourself or don't know yourself due to external or internal influences *can* have an upside; it's all about perspective. After a period of time, and some self-reflection and enquiry, we should be able to see the ways we have grown, or our further opportunity for growth.

For example, in 2021 I took part in *SAS Australia*, a reality TV show based on the special forces training program. I was really enjoying the course and, mentally, felt like I was doing well. However, I decided to leave the show voluntarily due to an injury. The morning I decided to go, I thought about my values. My value of taking care of my body helped me overcome my ego and influenced my choice to leave.

It took me months to get clarity on the positive evolution that came from my choice to withdraw from the show. Each week I would ask myself questions about the experience, and for months I didn't have any answers. Finally, the clouds parted, and I could see and feel all the growth and benefit from my time on the show as well as my decision to leave.

There are many reasons why you may feel like you have lost touch with yourself (if you have), such as friendship choices, addictions, distractions, unexpected misfortunes or mental-health struggles. Or maybe you're ready for change – to shed your old skin and move into the new. It doesn't matter where you are, what matters is where you're going. We are always changing and evolving, it's the nature of human beings. These changes can offer you opportunities to grow.

Can you try to view a setback as an opportunity to positively evolve? To see it as a beautiful blessing and a chance to grow into the best version of you? Losing touch set me on a quest of self-discovery. It showed me the value of being myself and compelled me to build a stronger connection with my heart.

~~

He forgot to ask what her favourite colour was. He forgot to unravel daydreams from his mind when she spoke to him. All she wanted was to be seen. To be asked what made her heart sing and her tears fall. One day, she stopped waiting by the edge of the ocean with her feet in the sand. She became her own adventure. She painted her room her favourite colour and wrote love poems about her heart's desires. She didn't need him anymore. She didn't wait for him to question what made her tears fall; she now caught them herself.

~~

PERMISSION TO CHANGE

Before I knew the magnificent power of being my authentic self, I felt like I had lost myself. I was ready for change; I left a long-term relationship and made a pact to myself to see the path ahead as a blessing. I set my intention and, by connecting to my *why*, strengthened my wish to evolve and step into my authentic self. The key was looking forward, not back, and finding peace with exactly where I was. Human beings are meant to change, but the way we live can often leave us feeling stuck. Some people may grow up with the same friends in the same town for most of their lives, but our spirit can blossom in any direction if we allow it to.

I left with a suitcase … I had no idea where I was going or what I was going to become, but I had determination. For the first time in a long time, I was on my own. I began to ask myself these questions.

- What do I love?
- What are my interests?
- What kind of friends do I want?
- What kind of community would I like to attract?
- Where do I want to live?

The next year, my journey of discovery led me to Byron Bay. I didn't know anyone but, as the months unfolded, I began seeking community, connecting with people via social media, trying new workout classes and looking for opportunities to make friends. I made sure to enjoy the newness and to treat each day like an open book. New discoveries and experiences excited me. The simple act of viewing getting lost as a place I could grow and have fun was a game changer. This experience shaped me and has influenced my life motto: to always keep a childlike vitality for life. Life is better when you keep things light and fun.

COMMIT TO COURAGE

Wait, but what if what I want to achieve scares the shit out of me? It's not about not being scared, it's about feeling your fear, then putting it aside and getting on with the task, having resistance and control over the fear – a commitment to courage. Time after time, I step forward with no damn idea if I can complete the task in front of me. What I do have a good idea about, though, is the power of my mind. I think to myself, *The only thing that is going to hold me back is self-doubt. If I believe I can do this, I have double the chance of succeeding.*

Believe in yourself and commit to fortitude. Fear and doubt will always simmer in the background – it is not something we can expel from our world – but we can choose to put fearlessness at the forefront. I like to say that fear is only useful if it teaches us something. You may wish to see if you have any limitations on yourself. Is the fear you feel old or new? Is it helpful or unhelpful?

If you are on the road of rediscovery, making a fresh start or ready to embrace change, trust the new journey. Celebrate and have fun. Discovering new things is electric. It's time to explore new paths and ways of living. Do things you enjoy: browse Spotify for new musicians, get coffee in a new neighbourhood, try an art or pottery class. Can you expand your perspective to see this new phase of discovery as fresh and exciting? Like the honeymoon period of new love? Go on 'dates' with yourself. All those new things and experiences that excited you about the beginning of a relationship – now, you get to do them with yourself. I take myself on dates every week, always switching it up. Some of my favourite 'Isabelle dates' are going to the farmers' markets, exploring a new bike trail, or playing my ukelele in a cool location.

Each sunrise brings a new opportunity – a light to guide you through any darkness. If you have recently come out of a difficult circumstance, lost touch or are just ready for something new, I want you to know that you are about to turn a corner. If you believe in yourself and use the practices from this book, a light will appear to guide you down the rainbow road of self-discovery.

~~~

Your past does not define you,
You define you.
Your decisions, actions and beliefs,
Standing up each day and creating who you want to be,
Your history doesn't write your story,
You write your story.

~~~

Practise
Forgiveness

Forgiveness allows us to move beyond what binds us to our past. Practising forgiveness opens the door to liberation. Feelings of pain, regret or sadness are valid when we are cultivating forgiveness, but holding on to these feelings can result in emotional self-harm. Acknowledge the feelings, learn from them and then let go.

The reality is that we will sometimes mess up or unintentionally hurt ourselves or others. The worst harm is not the event itself, but the way we grip onto these past experiences, beat ourselves up and create stress. To forgive is to let go. True wellness does not come from an internal environment that is tight and restricted.

Each time that I've forgiven myself, or accepted things that have happened in my life, I've felt lighter. The cool thing about forgiveness is that you don't have to wait. You can forgive *now*. Forgiveness allows us to cut the ties that limit the weaving of new webs. The webs that support our journey, catch our falls and encourage our growth.

The Power of Writing

I use journalling as a healing practice to navigate confusing or difficult experiences. I also write letters of gratitude and forgiveness. Writing helps me in my relationships with others. I have gained so much self-healing and growth from this simple healthy habit, and it is also available to support you. You can write letters about anything and to anyone. You don't have to give your letters to the person (you totally can if you want to, though!); what matters is that you're writing things down and handing your words over to the universe. You can write something and tear it up, or you might like to keep it. It doesn't matter what you choose to do with the words after you have written them, because the healing happens *during* your expression of writing. It's a process.

FORGIVING YOURSELF AND OTHERS

The work of Pema Chödrön has inspired me to stop ignoring my uncomfortable emotions, but to acknowledge and accept them. I like to view feelings of being unsettled as an opportunity to cleanse, like a python shedding its skin. I can feel and express my emotions to let go of what is not serving me. When I need to shed and let go, writing is the practice that benefits me the most.

One day when I was feeling like this, I picked up my journal and started to write. The words began to flow, and a river of clarity and understanding streamed through me. For the first time in years, I realised the energetic force of forgiveness. My pen scribbled like mad across the pages. Opening my heart and listening to my intuition led me to forgive myself for many things I'd never let go of. I'd been holding on to pain and past experiences perceived as failures or wrongdoings. I was healing my heart through my pen. I was forgiving myself for everything I felt I'd messed up on, and letting go of all the stored stress in my body.

After going through this process, my discomfort transformed into feelings of gratitude. I spent that afternoon at the beach writing thank-you letters to everyone who has supported me, guided me and been there for me during hard times. Some letters were to strangers, while others were to health professionals, family and loved ones. I also wrote a thank-you letter to myself, and even one to COVID-19!

~~~

Dear self,
I am grateful for your strength, gratitude and love.
You did the best you could in trying times, and I am so thankful for you.
You are enough.

~~~

Dear Izzy,
It's okay to lose balance. It's okay to feel sad and not good. To feel like you have lost touch with your strengths. But, all of these challenging feelings can teach you things if you let them. You are not alone; you have yourself. So, support yourself with the love you need. You can find the light through all the shit that hurts you; you will be okay. To fall is to teach.

~~~

~~~

Dear COVID-19,

You have hurt my heart. You have erupted hurt, fear, stress and grief among the collective. I see the lessons you are teaching us: walls of isolation building hours of internal reflection. But I need to tell you something! I might not know much about you, but I have some ideas. I understand the law of vibration. So, I vow not to be a victim. By making this choice, I'm helping you heal because I know your heart hurts too. I'm going to do all the things within your guidelines that make me blossom. Sing, dance, be among nature, read, learn and make home-cooked meals. I'm going to fill each of my days with all the things I love. I'm going to be happy. My daily intention, I hope, will cause a ripple of positive vibration. A ripple that, if others vow to make, may create waves. To stitch back our hearts. To stitch back our hands. We are one. I just wanted to let you know that I'm choosing to show up in joy and love. For you, me and the world.

~~~

The practice of letter writing has no rules or regulations. You can write about anything. During a forgiveness ceremony to myself, I wrote letters to everyone in my life who I felt like I owed an apology to. After the separation from my partner, I wrote him a letter that thanked him for the years we shared and the love he gave me. I included in this letter my intention and commitment to let him go. To cut the internal weavings that were left in my heart from those five years I shared with him.

Each time I have harnessed the power of writing letters, I have felt as if a ship's worth of weight has been lifted off my shoulders. Most of the time, no one sees the words I write. I finish the practice and hand my page over to the universe. Now and again, I'll feel a need to send the letter. When I do this, I decorate the letter with drawings and stickers before posting it.

I invite you to play with this healthy habit. Next time something happens or you feel like you need to say something to someone that can't be comfortably spoken, write them a letter. Need to forgive yourself for a mistake or an old relationship? Write yourself a letter. You don't need to carry anything that isn't serving you anymore.

BE COMPASSIONATE IF YOU MESS UP

There is a lot in life that we can't control, and there will be times when things fail and get messy. To be honest, if things were always rosy, then life would be pretty vanilla. Valuable lessons would not be learned. We would miss out on the bliss of the rise from a fall.

At some challenging moments, we can forget our healthy practices. Being a human means that no matter how hard we try, sometimes, even with the best intentions, we can still mess up. So, how do we respond when we fail?

I'm usually quite a cool, calm and centred person. My internal work provides me with a space to practise mindfulness, stay grounded and navigate difficult times with grace. Most of the time, it all goes to plan and I'm able to see the positive of a situation. I like to say, 'When shit hits the fan, you can dance through it or you can scream and cry'. Most of the time, I'm dancing. But I'm human and sometimes shit can really hit the fan and I scream and cry. But, guess what … that's okay. I don't sit in misery and beat myself up for not staying mindful, calm and collected. I use compassion to develop an understanding that sometimes it's okay for things to suck. There are moments when everything seems to fail. Living life in a realistic mindset allows for mishaps to occur. It's about doing your best in every moment, where possible, and letting yourself off the goddamn hook when you don't.

I find self-love the hardest when I feel like I have messed up. Learning from these experiences has shown me the importance of having kindness for myself and not sitting in regret for any 'failures'.

A practice that can help us when it all falls to shit is learning to be a friend to ourselves. Having compassion when we fall and keeping this compassion in mind when someone or something hurts our hearts. Loving through failure is a much simpler task if we have compassion for others, but it's just as important to show up in this way for ourselves too.

We can't always be happy and smiling. There will be times when we just feel terrible. There will be days or moments where things don't rock. This is where we bring understanding to how it's okay just to 'be'. Sometimes, all the work you do or your self-love will crumble. When this happens, the most valuable thing you can do is be okay with where you are; to cultivate compassionate contentment for this state of being and speak to yourself with understanding and acceptance. Tomorrow is a new day and a chance to dust yourself off and once again work towards becoming a better version of yourself.

It's okay to fail, as failure is a part of life. The important thing is *how* you respond to failure and the lessons you take away from it. Good can come out of all your mistakes if you look for the lessons.

'We do not receive wisdom,
we must discover it for ourselves ...
The lives that you admire, the attitudes
that seem noble to you, they have
sprung from very different beginnings ...
They represent a struggle
and a victory.'

– Marcel Proust

Part 5
LET GO
OF PAIN

Dealing with Physical and Emotional Pain

Healing can be a bit like changing your bedsheets – it's a pain in the ass, but it's got to be done and you will feel better for it. Pain and discomfort are inevitable in life. We might not be able to avoid pain, but we can choose how we respond to it. We can either focus on the bad or open up to the potential for evolution and wisdom.

MY EXPERIENCE WITH PHYSICAL PAIN

I've known physical, emotional, mental and spiritual pain. The hardest time was when my body crumbled when I was living in LA. It all began with a small pull in my right adductor muscle during a 21-kilometre half-marathon. Over the next 2 to 3 months I tried following a health professional's strength program, but the nagging hip and leg pain kept lingering. I finally gave in, stopped training and booked in to see another physiotherapist. During my assessment, we did some deep stretching into my adductor muscle and hips. This was when everything began crumbling. Within hours, I had debilitating pain in my hips and lower back. (I hadn't stretched my lower body for a *long* time based on previous health advice.)

I got back to my flat and things got nasty. My body went into total shock. I couldn't move from the immense back and hip pain. I spent 3 days crippled in bed. I know it might sound dramatic, but there were a few moments where the pain was so bad that I felt like I was dying. I called my mum and dad back in Australia and told them that I didn't think I would come out of this.

I eventually made it through those few days and started moving around again, but each day was a struggle. Trying to manage daily tasks was taking a toll. I needed to go home and was forced to leave LA. I was suffering mentally, physically and emotionally, feeling incredibly anxious, stressed and confused. At this point I'd been living with this pain for 10 months. Each night, I lay awake, worrying about what could be wrong with me. Arthritis? Lyme disease? Autoimmune disorder? Or was I just going crazy?! Physiotherapists kept telling me that I didn't need any scans, and to just keep doing the exercises prescribed. One professional even told me that he believed it was all in my mind.

I couldn't accept living with a condition where I could hardly function. I couldn't go on walks, see friends or do anything I loved. I felt lost. At one point, I was on my bedroom floor screaming in physical and mental pain. As I lay there, I realised what I was most afraid of: not moving. I was forced to face my fears.

I spent weeks in surrender. There was nowhere to run. During this time, I started to look inside myself. Through asking questions, art and journalling, I caught glimpses of what really mattered to me. I realised that I had to cultivate strength and ride my way out.

Things got worse before they got better. My pain became my identity for a while. It consumed everything I was. The more I gave it my attention, the more it consumed me. Each day I would worry, stress and beat myself up about what was wrong and I labelled myself as a permanent chronic-pain sufferer. I started to tell myself this was the state I was going to be stuck in. The labelling caused me more harm, and I started to believe my thoughts. Here is a diary entry from this period:

~~~

I didn't know someone as strong as me could fall apart as I have. Last night, I broke. My body hurts – it's cramping head to toe. I wonder if the tears will ever stop.

~~~

Eventually I booked in to get an MRI. This was a hard decision for me after being told for months by many professionals not to. My scans revealed some issues with my hip and spine. The doctors told me I needed surgery. I was 24 years old … I felt crushed.

I posted a photo on social media, sharing my pain story and the news about the surgery. I was surprised to receive a message from a woman who lived a few hours away. She put me in touch with her husband, let's call him Robert, who specialised in kinesiology and Neural Organisation Technique (NOT). Kinesiology and NOT are holistic healing treatments. They look for imbalances in the body and attempt to restore harmony. Rob told me that he believed he could help me. I expressed my gratitude to him but told him that I couldn't get off my bedroom floor, so I wouldn't be able to travel. Within 24 hours and the day before Easter, this incredible person turned up on my doorstep.

Still to this day, I cannot believe the professional care and grace he showed me during our session. He laid me down on his treatment table and pulled out his thick guide book. He treated me for hours on end, with only a few short breaks where I insisted I had to get off the table because of the pain. I decided to not take painkillers during this time because they made my head foggy. It was important for me to feel the connection with my body. I didn't want to numb out during the treatment. At times I was on my back, other times I was on my belly. His gloved fingers went in my mouth and around my eyes. I had to push on energy points on the front and back of my body. I have many distinct memories from this treatment. The right inside of my mouth and jaw was so tight. Releasing it felt like dragging a wrecking ball through the sand. We uncovered different layers of stress and trauma that were stuck in my body. This therapy helped to release stress in different disguises. Releasing emotional and spiritual pain offered me relief from the physical pain in my hip and back. I understand this kind of therapy might not work for everyone, but it worked for me.

My intimate dance with pain has shaped my core beliefs and philosophies on life and it showed me the power of natural healing. By staying open to receive wisdom and growth from the difficult times, I learned so much about the body as a whole.

STAY CALM AMIDST THE CHAOS

The more I grasped onto the pain, the worse it became. When something bothers us and we fuel it with more negative energy, we spark stress. This chemistry can cement the discomfort further into the body. The more attention we give to the unwanted, the more it becomes us. It's a challenge to relax among chaos, but relaxation is an ideal state to heal in.

EMBRACE DISCOMFORT TO EXPAND

We can view discomfort as a place from which to awaken. Trying to embrace what you feel can help you become more at ease. I believe that the tough moments can make us better people. Viewing my pain as a space for growth made me become more than I ever was. When I was forced to slow down and surrender, I was able to forgive and release emotions I had not expressed in years. I dove into this mindset of expansion with compassion and understanding, instead of punishing myself for the place I was in.

THE HEALING JOURNEY IS NOT LINEAR

It's important to remember that if you are on a healing journey, most likely it won't be linear, or smooth sailing. There may be bumps along the road – but you're still moving forward.

Physical, emotional, mental and spiritual pain are all connected. Any form of stress can drastically impact any experience of pain. Healing the pain in my physical body was like slowly peeling back layers of my emotional and spiritual self. Each month of the chronic pain, I would discover more twigs that were fuelling the physical fire. I needed to heal my pains of the heart – I had to forgive myself for my past and I had to release limiting conditions I'd placed on myself.

I now understand how my physical pain is connected to my internal world. My hip is still my weak spot, and if I'm somewhere I shouldn't be, my hip will often start aching. If I am stressed or not living by my truth, I can feel pain return. I had to shed a magnitude of emotional pain to relieve the discomfort in my physical body. Imbalance in one part of the human body can appear as a symptom in another. Everything is connected, so if you are experiencing pain in your body, it may be beneficial to look at healing on all levels.

FEEL THE FEELINGS, THEN LET THEM GO

What we resist will persist, and what we acknowledge, examine and deal with can cease to exist. When you feel uneasy, how often do you sit with your feelings? How often do you embrace what you feel and accept it? It's definitely not easy to sit with your feelings, I know. But it's worth trying. I know this practice has transformed my world and all my struggles.

In moments when feelings arise and you have the urge to avoid them, I encourage you to stop resisting. Can you find a way of being okay with everything you are feeling? Emotions are not outside of you. They are not something to be forced away. Once feelings are honoured, they are given the space to pass, and they will no longer tap on your door. But you need to embrace them, not ignore them, in order to let them flow out. By finding peace and being okay with your emotions, you may begin to understand them and let them pass by like the waves of the ocean.

The self-love mantra I find beneficial for arising feelings is 'let go'. For example, I may experience the feeling of loneliness arise. I don't avoid it or let it suck my energy in rambling thoughts. Instead, I breathe and open my arms. I let it surface, I give it space to be felt and then I chant the mantra, 'let go'. By breathing and letting go, I create a sense of flow. This process is not always instant, but it's a practice that helps me to dissolve discomfort.

You are the ocean not the waves

EMOTIONAL PAIN AND TRAUMA

In this chapter, I'm really grateful to feature Emmy Brunner. Emmy is a psychotherapist, hypnotherapist, coach, trauma specialist, author and CEO of The Recover Clinic, a family-run organisation for the treatment of trauma and mental health disorders. Here is a note to us from Emmy:

We all experience emotional pain as a result of the experiences that we have gone through as human beings. If our emotional pain is ignored or not acknowledged by others, it makes it very difficult for us to process it and to move on. So often we fail to recognise events as 'traumatic' and struggle to understand exactly what constitutes 'trauma'. When I talk about trauma in my clinic, I'm referring to any challenging event that has either happened to you directly or that you have witnessed – anything that has overwhelmed you, that your system couldn't handle or process and so has become an ongoing source of issues.

I believe that unprocessed trauma is the cause of what is often referred to as 'mental illness', and until people have learned new ways of coping with that trauma and processing the associated emotions, their symptoms will somehow still be serving a purpose and so they will continue to struggle with an internal critical voice and associated destructive behaviours.

Unprocessed trauma leaves us with a heavy sense of shame about who we are as people. We become trapped in a cycle where we are terrified of people really seeing us for who we are ... but are equally desperate to be seen and understood. In order to heal, we need to challenge some of these damaging shame-based beliefs that we hold about ourselves. When we start reflecting on some of the difficult experiences that we've had, we're able to consider how they have framed our beliefs about who we are and the story we've told ourselves.

I find these words so helpful, and I hope you do too. We can't go back and rewrite a story that has already been written. However, we can influence the narrative of our future. Many of us will experience some form of trauma in life. We can despise these events, but that attitude will not change what has happened. Have acceptance for the parts of the heart that hurt. It's okay to have places inside that don't feel okay. You can heal, and until then the lesson is about creating a safe space to sit in the dark. Remember that pain and trauma need to be dealt with rather than ignored and, as Emmy Brunner says, always put your recovery first.

Emotions and feelings swell, and we all have struggles. But we should try to lovingly accept where we find ourselves. This sense of mindful compassion is what builds the road to healing – to witness where we are without judgement in order to create a safe internal space that holds you when you feel sad. A space that doesn't punish you where your heart already stings. So, what does it mean to vow to respect yourself through all of your resistance and pain? Real growth! A warrior life! This is the beauty of embracing the quality of love in everything you go through. This, my dear, is the journey to building a home in your heart.

DON'T HIDE – ASK FOR HELP

Here is one thing I do know: expressing how you feel and not hiding the hard times is liberating. If you need help, support or assistance of any kind, don't be afraid to ask for it. I believe that vulnerability is one of the most beautiful qualities. You are worthy of receiving any care you need. You never have to go through anything on your own. As challenging as it may be at times, I encourage you to ask for help and seek support when you need it. Talk to your friends, family, doctor, therapist – anybody you trust and who can support you.

Being a warrior means continually fighting for your best life. It's about showing up and looking for places to heal in all that hurts and staying dedicated to your path of health and happiness. Your dedication and fortitude will not go unnoticed. And you don't have to go it alone.

RETREAT AND RECHARGE

When we take time to heal and focus on self-development, please know that it's okay to take a step back and retreat. You might like to decline some invitations to social events or choose to take some time off work (if you can). Sometimes the soul just needs a recharge. Give yourself the space to rewire and rejuvenate. It's okay to say no. Tell your friends or loved ones that you just need to lay low for a little. Taking care of your internal world is not selfish. In fact, it's an essential act of selflessness. By nourishing and caring for your own mental, physical, emotional and spiritual health, you will be able to be more present with those you love. You can give more love to others when you care for your own self-love. To restore is to bring back harmony. If you feel like you need to unplug, give yourself permission to take all the time and space you need. I do.

Natural Healing

There are different methods and ways in which we can heal. Love heals, embracing our authenticity heals, wellness practices – such as diet, yoga, acupuncture, meditation and breathwork – can all support healing. Understanding the different ways one can heal, including both Eastern and Western approaches, means that you are not powerless. There are ways you can support your health using both traditional and non-traditional methods.

There is an interesting analogy commonly used by medical practitioners when explaining a brain-chemical imbalance and the use of certain types of medications. When describing depression, they often say the brain is like a bathtub and the water is full of serotonin, otherwise referred to as the 'happiness hormone', but depression can feel like having leaks in the bath. Medication can be useful to help plug the leaks, which provides a base to build from. Therefore, medication becomes part of a treatment protocol. It is used to provide a healthy foundation so that the individual can implement other lifestyle habits, therapies and diet changes to support their healing journey. It's not a cure, but a support system.

When I was diagnosed with adult ADHD, I became intrigued about the use of orthodox medication for people with leaks they just couldn't patch up on their own. What I noticed is that the people who had the most success were those who used a combination of medication *and* healthy habits. For example, those who have high cholesterol are prescribed healthy dietary guidelines along with medication. Similarly, research on the treatment of ADHD reports that medication alone may be insufficient. Some of the non-pharmaceutical interventions (NPIs) prescribed to minimise symptoms consist of psychotherapy, exercise, coaching and dietary changes. If someone needs medication, it is used in conjunction with other NPIs to optimise treatment.

This is my take on the balance of pharmaceutical medication and alternative medicine: if medical intervention is needed to help manage your struggles, I like to see it as a tool in your toolkit; a sidekick that you can use for support among other things. I don't view medication as the cure, but a helper that can be used along with things such as adequate nutrition, movement, sleep and therapy.

Alternative or holistic medicine is a form of healing that considers the whole person – body, mind, spirit and emotions – in the quest for optimal health and wellness. Natural healing has been around for centuries and Native Americans, Chinese and Indigenous Australians are among the cultures that have used the power of natural healing methods to restore wellbeing.

Personally, holistic healing is what I always try first. Over the years, I have had the pleasure of trying different natural healing practices. Some methods have been as simple as meditating and using visualisation to go back in time and connect to my child self. By using my imagination, I have been able to give a younger version of myself essential needs like more love and support in places of lack. Doing this work benefits who I am today. It's quite amazing the ability humans have to self-heal. There are so many free practices you can implement into your life today. Below is one I really like!

You don't have to dive deep into healing with a practitioner or visit a fancy retreat. There is a way to add natural self-healing methods to your daily lifestyle. Maybe you can start to meditate, try breathwork (see page 208), visit a naturopath to get some herbs or see a psychologist. Once a year, I love to spend time cleansing my physical, emotional, mental and spiritual bodies with a detox. I love a sweaty evening infrared sauna or the high vibes I get from ice plunging or cold showers. I take turmeric as a dietary supplement and dedicate time out to rest and rejuvenate.

It's all about experimentation. Try a range of different healing practices until you discover what supports you best. The epic thing about this modern world is that we can access *both* traditional and modern methods for natural healing.

Try this

THROW A WORRY STONE

Find a nice location that's comfortable and safe enough to throw something. For example, at the beach into the ocean, by a lake or over a cliff ledge. Find a small rock or stone and hold it to your heart. Fill it with all the stuff you don't want to hold inside anymore. (This can be anything that's troubling you, such as mistakes, past experiences or feelings like sadness.) Once you have filled your rock with all your worries and pains, take a deep breath, throw it away and let all the shit you don't want to carry go with it.

Breathwork

Remember how we talked about the breath and mindfulness earlier in the book? Well, I'm going to talk about it again, but this time in relation to its healing effects. Nathan Gallagher helped with this chapter and he contributed some enlightening information.

Breathwork is a way to describe different conscious breathing techniques and exercises, which can be used for healing. Research published in the *Journal of Contemporary Psychotherapy* even speaks about breathwork as a treatment option for anxiety and depression.

Breathwork originated in different traditions around the world, but one of its pioneers in the West was German psychotherapist Wilhelm Reich. It has been used in many ancient practices such as yoga and the martial arts in China, Japan and Russia. My friend and breathwork facilitator Nathan Gallagher says that, 'Working with the breath can be likened to working with energy itself, which is also known as life force, *prana*, *qi* or "spirit energy" in different lineages'.

You may already have tried different breathwork techniques (called *pranayama* in yoga), such as *kapalbhati* or *ujjayi*. There are more than 50 different pranayama techniques alone. Nathan suggests adding some breathwork to your daily routine as a workout for your spirit, or diving into more therapeutic sessions for deeper healing.

THE POWER OF BREATH

One man has made breathwork very famous. His name is Wim Hof and you may have heard him referred to as 'The Iceman'. Hof has done some remarkable things by using the power of breathing techniques. After 30 years of society deeming him 'crazy' for being able to do 'superhuman' things, he has since become world-famous for the 'Wim Hof Method', which teaches people to carry out similar superhuman achievements. The method is based on three pillars: breath, ice and commitment. The breathing technique is used to increase oxygen and is therefore said to benefit energy, help reduce stress and to improve the body's immune response.

Hof's breathing technique has been proven by peer-reviewed scientific studies to show a diverse array of health benefits such as increasing immune cells in the body and decreasing inflammation (one of the main sources of disease). Personally, I view working with the breath as a fundamental base for living consciously.

THERAPEUTIC BREATHWORK

My first breathwork experience took place in 2017 during my 300-hour yoga and meditation teacher training, nestled in the jungle of Ubud, Bali. I was 5 nights into a 7-day detox program. Before the evening breathwork practice, I felt many emotions shifting and surfacing inside my body. I felt fragile and not up for the late session, but my intuition told me that I needed it. It was a guided therapeutic breathwork practice led by a lovely Australian woman. The open yoga studio was candlelit, with yoga mats and blankets set up in one large communal circle. Each student was instructed to lie down comfortably in a *savasana*-like position (lying flat on their back) on their mat. The instructor said there would be music and guided voice instructions. We were advised that the 'ceremony' was going to take a few hours and that we needed to stick to the instructed breathing method for the entire evening. She informed us that we might experience a range of strange, emotional or physical releases.

An hour into the session, my body started to shiver. I wanted to resist and pull out of the practice, but I knew I was avoiding something that needed to surface. I became braver and began to breathe deeper. The music gained pace, and I could hear tears and sounds from others in the room. Some people were crying and others were experiencing a bliss-like state. I committed to pushing past my fear, deepening my breathing pattern and opening to the unknown.

The experience I had in this session was remarkable. It started with a shuddering known as 'tetany'. Tetany often involves the hands and arms cramping up. As I moved through the physical layer, I began to feel the release of old wounds and feelings that were stuck inside my body and spirit. The emotions coming out were painful, physically and mentally. I kept breathing, choosing to stay open and push through my fear. I then had a breakthrough – the pain and discomfort brought a blossoming of self-love and acceptance I had never experienced before. Tears started streaming down my face as the years of pain from not loving myself surfaced and began to dissolve. For one of the first times in my adult life, I felt enough. I felt beautiful. I felt the immense joy of self-love.

To this day, I can still feel the essence inside me that bloomed that night. It's quite amazing the way breathing can help us move into a different state of consciousness, a space that allows our mind, body and spirit to heal.

I will never forget the song 'Bountiful, Blissful, Beautiful' by Bachan Kaur that was playing on that fine evening in Bali. This track now has a place in my self-love practice and I will often chant it in difficult times. You may find it useful to create a little self-love song or playlist of your own.

I've experienced a handful of therapeutic breathwork sessions since then, and each one has been unique. Breathwork can be used to heal traumas and deep stress in the body, but its power can also be harnessed as a daily wellness tool to increase wellbeing and reduce stress. Each breathwork session leaves me feeling lighter and with a greater overall sense of health and happiness.

Key Healthy Habit

BREATHWORK

There are many ways to practise breathwork. The first step is to bring awareness to your regular breathing pattern. Every person on this planet has a breathing pattern that is unique to them. Some people breathe shallowly, slowly, fast or deeply, whereas others hold the breath. Since we were born, we have all developed our own habitual breathing patterns.

According to Nathan Gallagher, different breathing techniques are like different tools in a toolbox that we can use as and when we need them. When beginning to use this healthy habit, start small and try a few different methods to see what works for you. I like to add breathwork to the beginning or end of my yoga or meditation practice for some healthy habit pairing (see page 126).

>>

Here are three of Nathan's simple breathing techniques that you can start today.

Exercise 1: Box Breathing
This practice is used by Navy SEALs for generating focused relaxation. (When I was on the TV reality show *SAS Australia*, I used this practice to help me focus during the physically and mentally demanding tasks.) Find a comfortable position with your spine straight – relaxed but sturdy. Inhale from the belly (see page 37) and exhale in a gentle, effortless and relaxed way.

1. Inhale for 5 seconds.
2. Hold for 5 seconds.
3. Exhale for 5 seconds.
4. Hold for 5 seconds.
5. Repeat for 5 minutes.

Exercise 2: 4–7–8 Technique
This technique is grounding and deeply relaxing – especially good for anxiety. Find a comfortable position either lying down, or in a meditation pose with the spine straight – relaxed but sturdy. Always inhale from the belly and exhale in a gentle, effortless and relaxed fashion.

1. Inhale gently for 4 seconds.
2. Hold the breath in for 7 seconds while intentionally relaxing all your muscles and allowing energy to sink down through the pelvis into the floor. Especially relax your shoulders and jaw.

3. Exhale for 8 seconds as you allow yourself to feel total relaxation. Allow your energy to fully ground and sink through you into the floor.
4. Repeat this for a few minutes. (If you have anxiety, try four rounds of this multiple times a day.)

Exercise 3: Coherence Breathing

This practice harmonises and balances the heart rate and nervous system. Find a comfortable position either lying down, or in a meditation pose with the spine straight – relaxed but sturdy. Always inhale from the belly and exhale in a gentle, effortless and relaxed fashion.

1. Inhale for 6 seconds.
2. Exhale for 6 seconds.
3. Repeat for 5 minutes minimum.

Part 6
CONNECT WITH THE WORLD

Connections and Relationships

We have cleared the mind, loved up our beautiful body and moved through some powerful new ways of thinking. Now, it's time to dive into the topic of connections.

You may be aware of how important it is to have positive connections with others, such as family, friends and loved ones, but have you thought about the transformational power of connecting with nature and the universe?

Healthy relationships are at the core of a fulfilled life. Positive connections offer support, encourage growth and help to reduce stress. However, harmful relationships can negatively impact our health, causing imbalance.

RELATIONSHIP WITH OTHERS

Take a look at the relationships in your life and contemplate whether they are positive or negative. I invite you to ask the following questions.

- Are any of my relationships causing me unnecessary stress and anxiety?
- Does my circle of friends support and uplift me?
- Do I have any relationships where I'm always giving and not receiving?
- What qualities do I most admire in my relationships?
- Who are my closest friends?
- What friends do I want to build closer relationships with?

Focus on cultivating uplifting and supportive relationships. To do this, define what qualities you need in your relationships and know what behaviours are acceptable and what behaviours are not. Once you have clarity on what's acceptable, you can draw a line that defines your worth and stick to these principles. This is your life and you get to make choices and decisions that support it. If particular people and environments are causing you distress, it's a great time to consider releasing these relationships from your life.

RELATIONSHIP WITH SELF

The most important relationship in your life is the relationship you have with yourself. Life is a journey of discovery; we are continually navigating the world and learning about ourselves. I believe the more time we spend strengthening the connection with ourselves, the stronger support we will have in times of need. People come and go in our lives, and there is only one person we will experience life with for certain: ourselves. It can take a while to get comfortable being alone but, over time, you can start to enjoy your own company (if you don't already).

There was a time in my life when I didn't like how I felt inside. I distracted myself, always moving, doing, listening and watching so that I didn't have to stop and feel. Doing things became a tool to try and escape. But the more I tried to run, the worse I felt. My anxiety soared, I experienced poor digestion and gut discomfort, and I was stressed. Eventually, I began to realise that this way of being wasn't working for me. I looked at myself hard in the mirror and made a choice to stop. From that moment, I chose to build a connection and relationship with myself that was greater than anything I'd ever imagined. Now, here I am. I spend a lot of time alone, as well as quality time with family and friends. I really value and treasure 'me' time, because it helps me to rejuvenate and self reflect.

Through this work and continually choosing to be kind to yourself, your world will evolve. You are the one who has to pick yourself up time and time again. Living an epic life represents the importance of building a strong and loving relationship with yourself. You need to have your own back.

Build a home within your heart

HEALTHY INDEPENDENCE

I believe the key to thriving relationships is loving and supporting each other through individual growth. To achieve this, we need healthy independence, or interdependence, which involves having a balance between time with others and time with self.

We can become dependent for many reasons. As children, we are dependent on our parents. If we don't grow up and build our independence, we can remain dependent. Or maybe dependency has formed during a long-term relationship where there was not enough individual authenticity. It's useful to note that being solely independent can also cause imbalance. This is where we find the middle ground.

Getting comfortable spending time alone is essential for personal growth. It supports self-love and provides space and time for inner reflection and to ponder and define your dreams, desires, wants and needs. I gain profound insight and intuition-based guidance when I am alone. If we are always around others such as friends, family or a partner, we can begin to depend on them and this can lead to feelings like stress and anxiety when we are required to be alone.

It's important to spend time with people you love but remember to put time aside to be with yourself. If you are worried about uncomfortable feelings arising when you're alone, remember that feeling is an essential human experience. Every feeling that arises is valid and, once honoured, can pass. If you feel as if you need people around all the time, now is a great time to ask yourself, *Why do I feel this need?* Then slowly challenge those behaviours by spending more time alone.

AUTHENTICITY

That word again! Authenticity in romantic relationships or close friendships will offer you support and guidance outside the walls you share with your partner or friend. When we fall in love, it's easy to get carried away and lose touch with friends as we find ourselves in a love haze. It's a magical thing to share a connection so strong that makes us want to spend every second with someone else. However, to thrive in relationships long term, it's good to maintain individuality and healthy independence. This means having friends that are outside of the relationship – people to count on in times of need. It requires work to continually remind ourselves of the importance of authenticity, but this is where we should *think big* and long term to gain clarity on *why* being authentic is essential. It's vital because no matter where you find yourself, if you nurture strong friendships, you will have people there for you no matter what happens in life. Healthy independence is essential for your personal growth. To thrive with another, we need to be able to thrive with ourselves.

If you are in a long-term relationship and don't have a lot of independence outside of the relationship, I encourage you to find new hobbies or activities that you can do solo. It could be an excellent time to get into a project that has always interested you – one that celebrates your authenticity. Take a look around your community and seek places to make new connections and friends.

GROWTH IN RELATIONSHIPS

Everyone we connect with in life has the potential to help us grow. It's all about perception. Finding the light in every situation allows us to discover wisdom in all places. For example, when reflecting on a relationship that may have ended in a difficult way, you can choose to fixate on ways of thinking such as, *I wasted so much time* or *I'm so stupid for being with them*, however, there is also the opposing way of thinking. So instead, you can cultivate more positive thoughts such as, *If I didn't have that experience, I would never have learned the valuable lesson of …*

The same opportunity can also be practised in our friendships. Since I began thinking this way, every one of my friends has taught me a valuable lesson. Opening myself up to gain inspiration from others has enhanced my outlook on life, and it may also bring insights into yours.

Challenging times in relationships will always arise. This is especially true in long-term romantic or close familial relationships. A partner, close friend or family member can shed light on places we were not aware we needed to work on, providing us with an opportunity to look at ourselves and grow. They say that the relationships in your life often reflect back to you like a mirror. Any difficulties arising in a relationship could be guiding you to look at parts of yourself that you could work on.

I always see it as a gift to discover more about myself. When I learn about a quality of mine that needs work, I try to be grateful and accepting of it. This insight provides me with work to do that results in becoming a better version of myself. For example, isolation during COVID-19 highlighted my lack of phone communication with distant friends and family. To work on this trait, I placed a sticky note on my car for a month, reminding me to FaceTime a friend.

ROMANTIC RELATIONSHIPS

As a teenager, I craved to fall deeply in love. I was fearless romantically. But when I entered my twenties, I noticed that I began to lose the courage to be open and love so limitlessly. When we grow up, past hurts and fear can get in the way and we can spiral into thoughts of the future, maybe even stopping the potential of falling in love before it has happened.

You might like to get curious about how you view your relationship between love and fear. Is love really scary? Or is the fear related to having to open and surrender to something so powerful, unknown and uncontrollable? I believe that love without limitations is the nature of our existence, but the mind likes to take over to try and protect us. When I got hurt romantically, I built walls to help 'protect' myself. After a few years of hiding behind my guard, while trying to heal from a past relationship, I realised that being closed was doing me more harm than good. I was afraid, but I knew something had to change. I had an opportunity to make a choice and said *let go* in my mind and, for the first time in years, I let myself receive a love-centred connection, and this was the moment when I genuinely healed.

~~~

I was closed.
Walls built tall and strong to protect me.
He looked at me and said, I've got you…

~~~

The work then becomes undoing, opening and trusting. Finding ways to practise the fearlessness we had when we were younger and loving and accepting ourselves the way we did as a child. You might like to ask yourself: *How can I open myself up to love, no matter what the outcome might be?* My quest has been to work towards unconditional love for others, myself, the animals and the world around me, and you might like to take some time to set an intention for your relationships too.

No matter where your heart sits, choose to love through fear. No matter what your past love story entails, trust that you are worthy. No matter what age you are or where you are on your journey, trust that you can meet someone who is right for you (if that's what you want). Be brave and continually remind yourself to stay open.

Looking for a partner or connection to fill a self-love void will not give you what you ultimately need. My personal experiences have taught me that we are more likely to attract love when we do the inner work and feel worthy just as we are.

Try this

SETTING INTENTIONS FOR YOUR RELATIONSHIPS

When seeking uplifting relationships, it's beneficial to ask yourself questions about your desires. Spend time journalling and thinking about what kind of person you wish to attract.

- What kind of partner do I want?
- What are my negotiables and non-negotiables in a relationship?
- What qualities do I appreciate in a romantic partner?
- How do I know they embody these qualities? (Make a list of the kind of behaviour these qualities relate to.)

It's one thing to know what attributes you would like in a potential partner, but *how* do they do these things? I'm talking about the evidence to back up these attributes, as actions speak louder than words. Also, if there are qualities you don't want in a partner, then define these to set healthy boundaries on what is best for you. Being a warrior means you don't settle for anything less than you deserve. Trust that the right person will come along when the time is right.

Sex

I'm sure by now you may be catching on to how energy exists in everything. As we learned earlier in the book, energy can be both masculine and feminine, and these Yin and Yang elements are in each and every one of us. When people have sex, a significant transfer of energy takes place. Learning this provided me with an insight into the way sex goes much deeper than physical intimacy and the pleasure side of things. In the past, I didn't understand why I often felt off after particular intimate experiences. I also didn't realise that I could use this knowledge of energy to enhance my health. Energy exists in all of us and in all things, and you get to make a choice about who you share yours with.

There is a difference between sexual desire and sexual intimacy. By understanding your desires and self-worth, you can decide how you want your sex life to feel. If you love a good one-night stand, that is no problem – as long as it's what you want ... everyone is different. Remember, you never have to have sex with someone if you don't want to. If you crave a sexual experience with someone you love, then I'm here to remind you that it's your choice not to have sex with someone until you find a person you connect with in this way. You never have to feel pressured to have intercourse because you feel like you 'should'. You never have to have sex for any external reason. *You* have the power to say no when you don't want it and YES when you do! It's your choice. *You* get to define what you want your own sex life to be. Your energy is sacred, and it's up to you to care for it wisely.

A NOTE ON 'THE END GOAL'

Disclosure: This perspective is purely from a personal, heterosexual point of view, so it may differ for others.

~~~

There seems to be a trait circling in the 21st century: THE END GOAL. But come on, some of us orgasm and some of us don't. But all of us should not have to feel a need to meet this expectation. There is nothing worse than the pressure to experience the end goal of an orgasm. It's all about the journey. If you do feel this pressure, then put the ball in your sexual partner's court. Have compassion, create separation and understand that it's not you. It's their experience, which could be influenced by many factors such as a cheeky ego, trauma, nervousness or past relationships. Speak to your sexual partner kindly and let them know that it's difficult to enjoy the process when there is pressure to perform. Pressure and stress are the number one orgasm killer; relaxation and fun is where it's at. Tell them that sometimes you may come, other times you won't and maybe you just never will ... But guess what? It's all okay. It's all normal. As long as you enjoy the process, that is all that matters.

~~~

EMBRACE YOUR SEXUALITY

If you feel uncomfortable about or have difficulty with self-pleasure, it might be time to bring out the sex toys, baby. Why? Because research shows that good old masturbation – AKA self-pleasure – can help relieve stress, reduce pain, increase energy, benefit your libido, strengthen your pelvic floor and even improve sleep!

Sex is a healthy part of life, so experiment and connect with your sexual body. I experienced embodiment and healing on so many levels when I began to embrace my body with self-pleasure. If you're interested in learning more about this, there are great 'positive sex' podcasts and many other online resources available out there.

As you work through the practices in this book on cultivating a more positive body image and a stronger sense of self-worth and self-love, this will likely have a positive effect on your attitude to sex and the choices you make.

Embracing your sexuality is a fundamental part of wellness

✳

Find Your Tribe

I was recently on my own on the other side of the world. I had no friends or family near me. I struggled to get access to nature and I was surrounded by concrete buildings in freezing winter temperatures. My vitality was diminishing fast. After 10 days alone, I felt isolated, dull and removed from the energy of a community.

It was the day of New Year's Eve, and I had just finished a 21-kilometre run with a gang of strangers. I found the event on Facebook and knew it was a positive 'butterfly effect' step to gaining connection. The run was amazing and, after it, I felt uplifted. Tired from the day, I spent New Year's Eve chilling in my accommodation, browsing the internet. I stumbled across a sober New Year's Day dance party the next morning. I was in! I bought a ticket and held on to the hope that the expression of dance would lift my spirits.

At 10 am on New Year's Day, when I walked into the room with my backpack full of water and protein balls, my sense of disconnect evaporated. I felt a warmth I hadn't felt in weeks. A smile beamed across my face, and I was welcomed into the club by sequined dancing legs. Finally, I felt I was in the right place.

This was when I realised that these conscious humans spreading love were my community. I hit the dance floor for a few hours surrounded by soulful people, shaking out all my worries and stress. I got a massage, drank mocktails and pulled an oracle card from a deck near the d-floor, which said: 'Find your light and stand in it'. This card reminded me of the importance of finding your community, your tribe – one that allows you to shine your light brightly.

I spent years searching for environments, events and a community where I felt I belonged, and it took me a long time to get there. When I came across the wholesomeness represented at Earth-friendly festivals in Australia, I felt at home. I now know that these little art and music festivals and the people who attend are my jam, my community, my vibe! This doesn't have to be what interests you, but I'm sharing my story in the hope that you will search for things and people that light you up. The best part about finding your community is that it is a choice uniquely individual to *you*. The people you resonate with can be entirely different from those you grew up with or work with. If you haven't found a good circle of friends or a healthy community, keep looking! Have trust that they are out there.

If you are looking to make new friends or connections, you should be brave and open to the possibility of meeting like-minded individuals anywhere. My mission to show up authentically and my search for new friends inspired me to create Facebook groups around Australia. The first group I made was in a small town in New South Wales. I grew up in this town but, as I changed, I lost touch with many of my high-school friendships. I had evolved, and so had my interests and passions, so I needed to expand my connections. Trust me, I had many setbacks before friendship success, but in true warrior-style, I kept showing up.

There were about six to ten people confirmed to attend the first two events I planned for my first Facebook group, and no one turned up. I was in the park on a Sunday at lunchtime, with platters of vegan food and wellness magazines I had planned to share with the new friend gang, but it was just me. I sat there alone that day and at a few following 'meet-ups' I planned. *What is true strength?* I questioned myself. True power meant that I wouldn't let little setbacks deter me. I kept showing up, trying to make new friends and working to inspire and help other people make conscious connections. These setbacks didn't make me feel sad. I didn't feel like a victim to my circumstances or like a loser. I felt empowered. And on the days that people did show up, my heart was warmed for weeks.

Don't give up on finding friends that uplift you. Don't give up on searching for a healthy community. They are out there! It's okay to outgrow old friendships – you change and your connections can too! Seek out new connections that support you and help you grow. Try new things, book into classes that interest you, join a Facebook group and keep having trust and the resolution to connect.

Spend Time
in Nature

You can do your crunches, eat your kale and meditate, but if you don't prioritise a connection with nature, an element will be missing from your overall wellbeing. Connecting with the earth and environment can help to heal you, support you and care for you.

Nature means everything to me. Spending time by the ocean or among the trees cleanses my soul and rebalances my body. It helps me to gain clarity on things that are important to me, such as my life's meaning and purpose. Nature's power is potent.

Thich Nhat Hanh, a Zen master and Buddhist, teaches that all our mental formations are organic in nature: 'We cannot separate human beings from the environment. The environment is in human beings and human beings are part of the environment.' Therefore, I believe that spending time in nature can also help us to find contentment in everything we experience. Compost helps to grow flowers and similarly our irritation or sadness can lead to a greater love and understanding of self. Reigniting our connection with nature can feel like reconnecting with a lost friend.

The conscious practice of taking time out in nature was vital in healing and rewiring my brain after difficult times. I can't imagine what I would have done without it. When I lose connection to the natural world around me, negative health symptoms surface. Re-grounding to Mother Earth is what helped ease my anxiety symptoms the most.

I feel safer among nature than I do in most places. I love to travel in my campervan, and often feel at ease because I know nature is with me anytime I need it. I gain strength from looking at nature. I can evolve and grow through even the darkest depths, just as the trees and plants do. Over the years, my connection has strengthened. I don't need to spend hours in nature, but I know that it's there for me.

～～～

I looked at the sea, and I saw
its limitless beauty inside of me.

～～～

The world has evolved, and so has our environment. Living in a modern world means many of us are walking around with a nature deficit. Studies show the benefits of spending time in nature range from increased energy and vitality to improved mood, sleep and a strengthened immune system. I've felt first-hand many benefits. When the natural world surrounds me, I feel nourished, calm and grounded. Connecting with nature is a natural, free and simple practice.

I want you to take an inventory of your lifestyle and look at ways to consciously connect with nature and Mother Earth. Can you spend time in places and environments that make you feel expanded and at ease? The natural world never disappoints!

I prioritise connecting with nature by going for walks outside or sitting on the grass for a few minutes at lunchtime. I love visiting new trails and waterfalls on the weekends, or swimming in the lake or sea. When I'm living in a city, I go to the park and meditate barefoot on the grass. (PS: Exercising in nature is like a double whammy – it can make you feel amazing.)

THE PRACTICE OF EARTHING

The most simple way to add this practice to your lifestyle is to walk barefoot as often as possible. If you can't take on some of your daily tasks with no shoes, then I recommend squeezing some extra time into your day or week to practise earthing. For this practice, you don't want to be walking on any concrete, cement or wood, as this will block the electric energy. You need to be on the earth. Take off your shoes and plant those bare feet on the ground. You can also lay down on the grass and ground your body to the earth beneath you. It's almost like letting your internal batteries recharge. I use visualisation and mindfulness during my earthing practice. I visualise the colours of the rainbow entering my body from the soil. They enter one by one, flowing through my body, helping to cleanse and rebalance me.

EARTHING

Earthing, otherwise known as 'grounding', is when you practise connecting your body directly with the earth. You can be shoeless or simply sit or lie on the earth. Earthing is essential in my lifestyle and I find it great for clearing the mind. When I practise earthing, I instantly feel a discharge of negative static energy. I feel calm and connected.

Earthing can be done anywhere in the natural world. Can you visit the ocean, or is there a nature reserve near your house? Can you sit among the trees on your work break? Can you do a nice hike on the weekend? Look at your weekly schedule ahead of time and see if there are opportunities to add in time to connect with nature.

Soul and Spirituality

You have an inner light that desires to shine beyond any external or internal confines. I find that connecting to my soul and spirit makes me feel free and in harmony with the universe. There are many practices we can use to help us dive into our internal light. Through self-love, natural healing, forgiveness and introspection, we can begin to see how we are beyond the external body. Connecting with your soul and spirit can help you to live an epic life. Here are some ways to strengthen the connection with your soul.

- Meditate.
- Spend time in nature.
- Ask internal questions.
- Connect with your heart.
- Journal.
- Ask for signs and guidance from the universe.

CONNECTING WITH SOMETHING BIGGER

To me, spirituality is about believing in something bigger than yourself. I feel we are all connected to 'the source'. But what is it? There are a number of ways we can describe 'source' – here are some generalised dictionary definitions.

- A place, person, or thing from which something originates or can be obtained.
- One that initiates.
- One that supplies information.
- The place something comes from or starts at.
- The cause of something.

'Source' can also be known as 'the universe', 'the divine' or 'god'. Your connection to something bigger can be represented in many different ways. I understand the source as the place we came from, where life originated. Some of us may think that if we don't believe in god, then we can't be spiritual. However, I don't believe this is true. I feel it's beneficial to find a spiritual practice in life, no matter how small. It can be a practice of meditation or yoga, or something as simple as giving thanks to the universe, Gaia (Mother Earth), the source or a personal god or guru. It's about finding things that help you feel connected to something bigger. A connection to something greater can be as simple as seeing beyond the external body and feeling the essence of the soul and spirit within everything and everyone.

You can have your own unique definition of what is sacred to you. Just know that you are guided and have support from the universe. Understand that you are greater than anything you do or the way you look. You're connected to something bigger – a living spiritual energy. Have trust in your journey through life. Harmonise with the universe, have faith and always listen to your intuition and heart. You are not alone. The universe will support you. Others are here to support you. We are a collective. You have guidance to call upon any time you are in need.

Connect with the Universe

There are many ways to connect with the universe, such as using channelling techniques, intuition and meditation, as well as oracle cards, crystals and tracking the moon cycle. Even if you don't believe in spirits, angels or gods, you may find other uses for these tools. For example, oracle cards can be an excellent resource for navigating difficult times, whereas the moon cycle may provide you with more insight and understanding into your hormonal and mood fluctuations. Here are some of the ways I connect with the universe. Experiment and find what works for you. These practices offer me a sense of support and comfort, of always being connected with the cosmic world.

INTUITION

I view intuition as an internal 'knowing' that stems from within, from a universal connection and truth. Listening to my intuition feels like following the vibrations of the universe and tuning in with the cosmic compass. I like to describe it as a gut feeling deep in my belly, like the tingles that make you stop in your tracks before doing something, the signs and signals that help you to find a path forward.

As you have probably noticed, I am guided by my heart and intuition in life. Intuition is the reason I'm here writing this book – remember, it all started with that flyer! However, along the way, I did temporarily lose touch with my internal compass and learned many lessons. Battling with my mental health, my insecurities led me to stop listening to my inner world. I felt like I needed external input for all my decisions and choices. The first step to rebuilding my intuition was cultivating self-love. The hard work began to pay off, and I was growing and evolving. Embracing my authenticity and individuality set me free. I became a warrior woman. Living this way made me realise that if I'm completely unique, then my decisions must be unique. I decided to try an experiment – to stop asking others what they thought and to start trusting what I felt. Man, it was hard at first. But the more I listened, the stronger my instincts grew and I began to tune in to my body. This experiment helped me to strengthen my intuition.

The more you practise connecting with your intuition, the easier it will get. Intuition is often the first instinct (feeling) you get before the analytic mind takes over. Play with tuning in! It can be a fun process to develop your connection with internal universal wisdom.

If you're someone who often seeks reassurance or advice, can you try an experiment to stop asking others for answers? Can you tune into your own feelings instead? The more we tune into our intuition (which also contains our vibes and energy), the greater our chance of attracting what we want. The first step in involves listening to your internal world. By mindfully pondering, *What am I feeling? What are my senses showing me? What is this feeling telling me? What choice do I want to make?* Step two involves taking action. It's one thing to feel the signals your intuition sends you, but then you should act on them.

Tips on Intuition

- If something doesn't feel right, then speak up.
- If you have a craving to learn something new, then take the leap!
- If your internal compass is waving red flags at one of your relationships, then investigate.
- Often intuition doesn't correlate to logic, however research says it may be 'the highest form of intelligence'.

You might be wondering *why* your vibes and connection with the universe matter. I have to tell you something … The universe doesn't miss anything! Nothing goes unnoticed. Understanding this little secret can give you the power to attract more of what you want in life. Sometimes it's not so magical, though. You can also attract unpleasant situations if you're not careful about your vibes. I believe it's all to do with the law of vibration and attraction. Be conscious of your connection with the universe and tap into its power any way you can. The more we prioritise internal work and become conscious of our thoughts, beliefs and actions, the more we can begin to manifest what we truly desire. Your vibes (aka your energy) have the potential to lead you on a rewarding path. Focus on what you wish to create. If you want to kick ass, spend time being courageous and mastering your crafts, your mindset matters! Remember, *what you think, you become.*

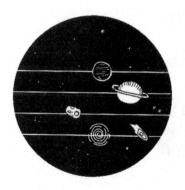

MOON CYCLES

The magical moon. I was intrigued to learn about the moon cycle when I found myself in a *deep* research backtrack on my computer. It was like one of those moments where you go on Instagram to check something and realise 45 minutes later that you're 15 pages deep in someone's 'gram account. My 'How the hell did I get here?' moment was on a full moon many years ago. I felt extremely wound up and

waning crescent

third quarter

waning gibbous

full moon

waxing gibbous

first quarter

waxing crescent

new moon

impulsive, craving to book an erratic last-minute trip overseas. Until … my research uncovered something bigger influencing my impulsive nature. Indeed, most of my 'crazy', impulsive desires seemed to fall on the full moon. I then became interested in learning about the moon and the impact it has on human beings. A general understanding of the moon and the lunar cycle enabled me to alter my lifestyle accordingly. Aligning with the moon cycle benefits my health and offers me a simple way of connecting with the universe.

Moon Facts

- The moon is estimated to be 4.527 billion years old.
- It takes about 30 days to cycle through all its phases.
- There are 2 weeks between the new and full moon each month.
- The moon dictates the push and pull of the tides. Humans are roughly 60 per cent water, therefore our bodies and emotions are greatly influenced by the moon.

The lunar cycle sketch opposite shows different phases of the moon. Now, I'm definitely no astrologer or moon guru, but here is some knowledge and simple tips that work for me on integrating the lunar cycle into my lifestyle.

Lunar Lifestyle Tips

- Download a moon app on your phone to keep track of the lunar cycle.
- Rest and cleanse on a new moon. This phase offers you a clean slate. It's the perfect time to plant the seeds of what you want to cultivate. Take time to set goals and ponder your dreams.
- The moon's waxing phase brings Yang energy, which is related to building, implementing and taking action. It's a great time to manifest things you desire!

- The full moon is when everything comes to a head, such as all the seeds you planted earlier in the cycle. It means high energy and results. It's the head of the storm and is a good time to burn off unwanted physical or emotional energy with a workout or dance. I love practising 'earthing' on a full moon.
- The moon's waning phase brings Yin energy, which is an ideal time to rest, retreat, recover and refresh. This phase supports self-care (I like to use my favourite body scrubs), cleansing, cleaning and time connecting with yourself.

USE CARDS TO HELP YOU CONNECT

I'm crazy for tarot and oracle cards. They inspire me, open my mind and help me to navigate crossroads in life. To me, they represent a way to deal with difficult times or further enhance my evolution. Cards are a simple way of connecting with the universe, higher spirits and angels. Even if you don't believe in higher beings, cards can help guide you through difficult life experiences, offer you a fresh perspective and outlook and expand your mindset. I don't go anywhere without a deck of oracle or tarot cards. These magic little helpers bring clarity to my life. The rad thing about cards is that you can take them anywhere. You can keep your deck as a sacred practice for yourself, or you can do readings for loved ones, friends or family members. You can draw cards as often as you like or just keep them for special occasions. It's your epic life.

- Tarot cards are not about black magic.
- They do not predict your future – that power lies in your hands only. They are for guidance.
- All you need in order to interpret tarot cards is your own intuition.

Cards

Tarot and oracle cards have been used for centuries. They are decks of cards that come in many different styles. Each variation serves a different purpose and each card offers a different message. When choosing your first deck, listen to and trust your instincts. Don't worry if you don't know how to use them, as all decks come with an instruction manual. There is also heaps of information about them on the internet.

Here is my perspective on the differences between the two main variations of cards.

Tarot – An original style of 78 cards that follows a set structure. They're a little more complex than oracle cards, and are typically used by expert readers. Tarot cards can be used by anyone, they just take a little more time to learn about and interpret. I typically use tarot cards to offer guidance on bigger life events, or when I am at a crossroads, due to their complex nature, but they can also be used daily.

Oracle – Oracle cards are more varied from the set structure that tarot cards provide and are the cards I use most often. There is more freedom to their interpretation and use. They can contain a range of different card numbers and you can even create your own deck!

Part 7
UPGRADE YOUR LIFESTYLE

Your Daily Routine

A core routine is developed by consistency. This consistency is doing things around the same time most days (when possible). The body thrives on routines. When it is provided with a rough sleep and wake schedule, it relaxes and can feel at ease. Did you know that we all have a 24-hour internal clock called the circadian rhythm? Maintaining a consistent circadian rhythm can improve general health, and it will help you to feel more balanced in your mood, metabolism and energy.

I encourage you to take a look at your core routine and daily habits – are they helping your lifestyle or hindering it? Is there an opportunity to create consistency in what time you go to bed and wake? Can you use practices to restore balance in the body to help it feel relaxed? Relaxation is key to healing, and we need to harness any opportunities we can to bring back this sense of tranquillity. Now is the time to create rituals and routines that are unique to you – a simple daily structure to help you feel your best. Question: *What makes you feel relaxed?*

An example of a simple daily routine is as follows: Waking when the sun rises, practising a 10-minute unique daily habit. Eating meals around the same time each day to regulate energy and metabolism. Being in bed and sleeping around the same time every night.

As humans, we're always looking for the 'fix' or grasping onto the idea of reaching or becoming something better. Even if we momentarily find it, there will always be a time when we are thrown into anguish. Nothing is fixed in life; we cannot predict the future or create walls to keep everything 'safe' just how we like it. We can try to build or seek our sense of comfort, but what happens when, once again, the proverbial tide washes in? The tide of job loss, injury, disastrous events, sadness, a breakup or a pandemic. What happens when we fixate on the pot of gold and arrive to find that it's not there? Instead, we can look at finding contentment in ourselves and our lives, and create a sense of harmony in the things we can control.

MORNINGS

Take a moment to envision 'Olivia' and the impact that mornings can have on our lives … Olivia awakes at 6.30 am to a buzzing phone alarm. After a few snoozes, Olivia starts scrolling through Instagram and a few of the images trigger her feelings of unworthiness. Feeling disheartened, she climbs out of bed and goes to the fridge. Olivia grabs some food and scoffs it down as she gets ready for work. Every item she looks at in her wardrobe annoys her. Feeling angry and frustrated that nothing looks 'good' on her, she simmers in feelings of poor body image.

But what if Olivia started her day in *action*, not *reaction*? It's the same morning. Olivia's phone alarm goes off. She quietens the alarm and sees the *meditate* reminder on the screen. She clicks on a guided morning meditation track saved in her phone and meditates. The first 10 minutes of Olivia's morning is spent easing the mind, breathing and connecting with her body. She feels grounded and calm. Olivia climbs out of bed and pours a glass of water, puts on her favourite music and gets ready for work. She gets dressed and looks in the mirror. Olivia's attitude is grateful – she reflects on how lucky she is to choose what she wants to wear to work every day.

This is the same day and the same person. Your world is a product of your actions. If you want to change your day, I encourage you to change your morning.

We don't and can't always have fabulous days, as we can't control what happens in life. But your morning routine is something you *can* control. There are no distractions and influences from the world. It's a time just for you. Can you use the first few moments of your day to create a stream of positivity like the 'butterfly effect'? Even if that just looks like taking 5 minutes in bed when you wake up before the rest of your household does. Cultivate a morning ritual that is achievable and realistic for you. The intention is what matters most.

I invite you to get curious about your mornings. What's the first thing you do when you wake up? Can you remove a possible negative trigger by not checking your phone immediately? Do most of your morning practices uplift you? Or is there a space to create a healthier morning routine? Can you implement rituals you enjoy into your AM hours? For example, meditation, dancing, breathwork, music, yoga, journalling or reading a short chapter from a book? Every sunrise is an opportunity, and it's my favourite time to set myself up for my day.

♡ *Things I am grateful for today ...* ♡

SLEEP

The same positive outcomes can exist when you have a nourishing evening ritual. Creating a conscious PM routine can improve your sleep, which can enhance your health and your happiness. Everything is connected, so if you improve your sleep, you improve your world.

Sleep quality and quantity is crucial to kick ass in life. Adequate sleep can improve cognitive function, whereas a lack of sleep can negatively impact our health in ways such as poor blood-sugar control, increased inflammation and cortisol (the stress hormone), unbalanced moods and an increase in leptin (the hunger hormone). A 2009 study found that an irregular sleep schedule correlated with a lower average sleep time per day, and may result in poor sleep quality. Regularity in your sleep and wake routine can drastically help sleep quality. Research shows that most people need at least seven hours a night. I find it beneficial to sleep seven–nine hours each 24 hours.

Sleep Tips

- Minimise screen time in the evening.
- Don't over-caffeinate your body throughout the day.
- Try to avoid hard workouts 3 hours before sleep.
- Reduce stress with grounding practices like meditation and journalling.
- Calm yourself with a lavender essential oil (or other relaxing oil of your choice) before bed.
- Reduce sensory influences by making your sleep environment as dark and as quiet as possible (sleep masks and ear plugs are great for travel).

Rising early in the morning can improve sleep quality by syncing your body clock with the Earth's natural circadian rhythm.

MAKE IT SACRED

A great way to make morning and evening routines stick is to make them sacred. You can do this by making sure you *enjoy* your personal ritual – and if you don't, then add some fun to it. Try slowing down and staying present during your AM and PM habits. My daily rituals and routines feel like a form of self-care. Here is an exercise I like to do when creating a routine, which begins with asking myself: *What are my rituals?* I then make a list of regular activities I do that make me feel good.

AM

- Rising with the sun.
- Practising affirmation.
- Moving my body.

PM

- Having quiet time before dinner.
- Journalling.
- Doing art or playing music before bed.

It doesn't have to be complicated. You don't need to have an over-the-top routine with a long list of shit to do. Just keep it simple. Start with one sacred act and, if you want, increase from there. Focus on creating a sense of harmony in your wake and sleep transitions.

Be Creative

You are a creative soul, but maybe you just don't know it yet. Yes, each one of us has a place inside us where we can express creativity. Want to know the secret to expressing your creativity? Getting out of your own way and not letting false limiting beliefs and thoughts tell you that you're not creative. That's it!

I'm talking about creativity here as an individual expression that enhances your health and wellbeing. Doing something or creating anything that comes from a part of *you*. Finding and expressing your creativity is an epic and exciting journey and it can bring joy and colour into your world. It might even change your life, like it has mine. Creativity is any type of artistic expression and occurs in many places, not just in the obvious arts and crafts. It's all about approaching things with curiosity, non-judgement and experimentation.

There are no limitations. You can express creativity in anything that appeals to you, such as art, dance, cooking, yoga, surfing, music, making movies, mood boarding, journalling, photography, writing, sewing, arranging plants or watching YouTube videos in order to learn a new craft or hobby. The possibilities are endless! Creativity is a form of soul expression. It's one of the best feelings in the world – like an internal explosion of goodness. It doesn't matter if you aren't 'great' at it. What matters is that you enjoy it.

Before we go on, I should remind you of something important: Watch out for the cheeky creativity blockers that come in the form of comparison and judgement. You are unique, therefore how you express your artistic style will also be unique. Check in with your thoughts and watch out for comments such as, *Oh, I'm not good like that*, or *I can't do that.*

Creativity has nothing to do with being 'good' at something, so just do whatever you want!

When I first started painting, I let self-judgement get in my way. I kept getting frustrated that my watercolours weren't 'good'. I then thought, *Aha, this art form is an opportunity to challenge the part of myself that wants things to be perfect.* These days, watercolour is an art form that helps me to embrace flow and cultivate freedom.

Try expressing more creativity, and if you're already quite creative, then maybe it's time to experiment with something different. We are trying to find something that spills out of you and makes you feel so damn good. Believe it or not, one of the key pillars eating psychologists work on with clients to heal unwanted food habits is *creativity*. Creative arts therapy is an approach used by many health professionals in the treatment of eating disorders. People who report increased eating disorder symptoms also report reduced flexibility. Thus, the correlation between creativity and healing could be due to the way art helps to express feelings and emotions, as well as challenge perfectionism and decreased flexibility. Yes, this is why creativity rocks and should be prioritised.

Baby, it's time to start having fun and experimenting with your creative side. If you don't already express your creativity, now is your time. You might like to ask yourself the following questions.

- What sparks my passion?
- What do I want to create?
- What do I enjoy making?
- What makes me feel alive?
- What interests me?
- What inspires me?
- What new skills would I like to learn?

Ponder these questions and begin to discover new things. Write them down in your journal and create space in your week to try something new. Throughout this journey, remember to get out of your own way. Don't worry if you aren't 'good' at something – it's not useful to compare yourself to others or an idea of perfection. It's time to start enjoying the magic and uniqueness of being *you*. Personally, this week I am going to learn a new hip-hop dance via YouTube, and I'm going to add my own flair and have fun!

DAILY INSPIRATION FOR CREATIVITY

Step 1: Be present in the moment. If you're caught in the past or the future, you will be removed from what is right here and now. How can the people you interact with or the things you witness inspire you if you aren't in openness to receive their vibration? Staying present and open can help us gain creative inspiration from our everyday environment.

Step 2: Seek inspiration! With gratitude at the forefront, witness your world with awe. Can you stop to notice how beautiful the sky is or to contemplate the pure joy and freedom that radiates from children on the beach? What about the magic colours of the sunset? This, my friend, is inspiration. Being present to notice the world around you. Let yourself be affected by the way light, love and the beauty of colour shines through the world. All of my creative inspiration comes from my daily life, by experiencing and seeking to be positively influenced by the world around me.

START NOW

I know creativity is hidden within you, and probably more than you ever could have imagined. Don't wait to start expressing your creativity, be creative now! From this moment on, can you find places to express creativity? If you can put some time aside to try some new things, amazing. If your schedule doesn't allow time to find new hobbies, then begin to add creativity into things you are already doing – arrange your salad attractively on your plate, or make fun breakfast bowls. Think of how you can be creative in everything you do, no matter how ordinary the activity.

'Why waste time proving over and over how great you are, when you could be getting better?'

– Carol S. Dweck

Creativity in Everyday Moments

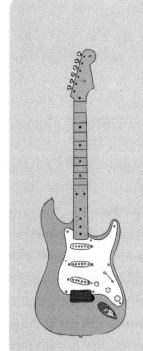

Creativity can come from anywhere. Doodle in a sketchbook. Ponder imaginative narratives or fairytales. Add some quirk and colour to your cooking. Write poems or collect flowers and press them in a book. Leave a beautiful pattern of shells on the beach. Start a new instrument or make clay figurines. Find as many little opportunities to add creativity to your everyday life. You don't have to only have one place to express your creativity. You can add its essence into many places.

Live Naturally

Undesirable chemicals and substances in your food, skincare, personal care and home products can have adverse effects on your health. After years in the modelling industry, I was led to believe that I needed to use commercial products containing harsh ingredients to avoid breakouts. Well, years on, instead of using those pricey (and often problematic) beauty products, I use natural alternatives and my health and skin have never been better.

Choosing to use cleaner products (or, even better, your own homemade versions) in your lifestyle is not limiting. The possibilities are endless. For example, I use natural cinnamon toothpaste, and mix bicarbonate of soda (baking soda) with white vinegar to clean my kitchen. I make body scrubs from recycled coffee grounds and moisturise my skin with coconut oil or cacao butter. The good thing about this modern world is the internet. It will provide you with free ample resources and recipes for going toxin-free.

Skin is the body's largest organ and it is said to absorb up to 60 per cent of the ingredients we put on it.

Did you know that if you tape raw garlic to your skin, then a few hours later you can taste it? Yes! So, everything you put on your skin has the potential to impact your health internally and externally. Harmful ingredients can influence many unwanted health symptoms such as skin conditions, hormonal dysfunction and an imbalance in vital organs. Natural beauty, personal care and home products are better for the environment, the animals and your health and wellness. All the small things add up. When I removed unnecessary chemicals from my lifestyle, blood tests confirmed that my liver and detoxification pathways improved.

Here are the most common nasties to try and avoid in your products. Scientist David Suzuki calls them the 'Dirty Dozen' and they are: BHA and BHT, coal tar dyes (colours listed as CI followed by a 5-digit number), DEA-related ingredients, dibutyl phthalate, parabens, parfum (aka fragrance), PEG compounds, petrolatum, siloxanes, sodium laureth sulphate and triclosan. Make sure you check the ingredients of a product before you buy.

HOW TO EMBRACE A NATURAL LIFESTYLE

- Start small. Each time you run out of an item, swap it for a cleaner alternative without the unnecessary chemicals.
- Before you use a product on your body, do a patch test by applying a small amount to your skin to check for reactions.
- Make your own products from food or ingredients found at a bulk food store.
- Less is more: you don't need ten skin care products, just find two great ones.
- If it looks or smells synthetic and over-perfumed, avoid it.
- Be a conscious consumer and do your research to make

sure you are buying the right items for you. Don't get fooled by every 'natural' label. Check the ingredients list. There are some great apps and websites to make this process easy.

NATURAL BEAUTY SECRETS THAT WORK FOR ME

Experiment and try different things to find what you love. Making your own beauty and health products is fun, cheap and creative. Try to think of it not as doing more, but as undoing and getting back to basics. Less is more. (Of course, even some natural ingredients, such as essential oils, can be quite active and may adversely affect some people, so do a patch test or watch out for reactions.)

- Watered-down apple-cider vinegar makes an epic toner for your face.
- Cacao butter is the most amazing body moisturiser. I buy it online or from a bulk food store and rub it on after a shower (a large block lasts me 6–12 months!).
- Coconut oil can be used as mouthwash, moisturiser and make-up remover.
- Avocado, honey and oatmeal make a dream face mask.
- Cafes often give away recycled coffee grounds that you can mix with coconut oil for a natural body scrub. I also love to exfoliate with raw sugar, or sand when I'm in the ocean.

BE LIKE BAMBOO!

A wholesome lifestyle can provide freedom if we integrate practices and sustainable ways of living that allow us flexibility. There was a time in life when I wasn't like bamboo (aka flexible). I was like a steel rod, caught in strict rules and regimens that did not allow flexibility. Suddenly, when my environment changed, my inability to bend caused me stress and anxiety. One of my dear friends looked at me and said, 'Iz, you need to be like bamboo'. He inspired me and

I began to ponder how I could implement the wisdom of being flexible like bamboo into my lifestyle.

I created this bamboo motto that changes and evolves as I evolve. You may like to create your own epic life or bamboo motto.

~~~

Be like bamboo.
Set goals but don't become stuck.
Define where you want to go but don't limit,
Be strong and compassionate,
Grounded and open,
Confident but humble,
Great and modest.
Work hard, rest often,
Grow and always bend.

~~~

Your healthy lifestyle should enhance your life, not limit it. Applying the wisdom of bamboo to a healthy lifestyle represents the ability to bend but not break. I encourage you to be grounded yet flexible. Living like bamboo will help you to adapt and adjust to different places, environments and people in life.

True wellness is found in flow and sustainability. This is why it's important to create a healthy lifestyle that is flexible. Develop strategies and practices to fall back on when you need to adapt. Be open to change. Create methods and nourishing practices that can be implemented into your lifestyle anywhere, any time. Travelling and can't access fresh food? Pack some dried greens superfood supplement. A busy work week without time to work out? Do 20 burpees or squats during your break. Be dedicated to growth but don't forget the importance of self-love through the hard times. Fall down, forgive yourself and pick yourself back up.

Avoid Sensory Overload

We are bombarded every day with mild forms of stress via our senses – smell, touch, taste, sight, hearing. Bright artificial lights, technology, loud sounds, synthetic smells and pollution can all impact on your energy, mental clarity and sleep. Try to be conscious of your environment and the places where sensory stress and toxins are leaking in. Here are some ways you may wish to balance your sensory environment:

• Spend time without music, television, radio or podcasts.

• Avoid the use of screens after sunset.

• Turn all of your electronic devices to night mode in the evening.

• Avoid white lights. Install red or orange globes in your home to use after the sun goes down.

• Limit scary television, movies and violent media.

• If you exercise with music, try to turn your headphones off for the last 10 minutes of your workout.

• Take a look at the environments that trigger you to eat junk food. For example, while watching stressful YouTube videos or consuming types of media that make you feel inadequate.

Start Your Epic Life Today

We don't live in a fairytale, and transformation doesn't happen overnight. The nature of life is unpredictable. Just when we think we have a hold on things, a curve ball comes along. But without this unpredictability, life wouldn't be as epic. The curve balls contain lessons – sometimes they smack us in the head and hurt, but they always make us stronger.

So fuck waiting to do the things you want to do, stuff waiting to create the life of your dreams – start living it today! You don't have to be anything more than you are right now in order to start. Ask yourself, *What is one small thing I could do today that would have a positive impact on my life and health?*

In this book I have spoken about how you should live like your future self, today. That's the way you get there, by making decisions and taking actions today that align with your future self. We've learned that to transform the way we view our body and our relationship with food, we need to find love and acceptance for ourselves and wherever we are on our journey. We need to have compassion for ourselves and our difficulties, and forgive ourselves for past mistakes and learn from them.

Limiting ourselves and delaying our journey towards an epic life can also be seen in the following language.

- 'I'll start Monday.'
- 'That can be my New Year's resolution.'
- 'After the holidays, I'll eat better food.'
- 'I'll wait until summer to improve my health.'

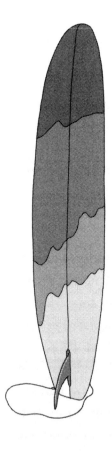

Create the future feeling inside yourself this very moment. If you start trying to live the life you want to have *today*, you can begin to reap the benefits immediately. Right from this moment, you can make a choice. Even if it's a super-small decision, it won't go unnoticed. It's time to take action, because life is too short.

If you want to be happy, start creating ripples of happiness and joy inside yourself by doing things you love. If you want to love and accept your body, start to celebrate and be grateful for how your body is today. If you want to go out dancing, *go dancing*. Action is the first step of change, and it's also a simple way to change your vibration. You only have one life, and it's up to you to make it an EPIC ONE.

Make Everything Fun

I just got back from a surf. Not the kind of surf you see in magazines or at the beach during a boardriders' competition, but the kind of surf where sand is everywhere, your swimmers end up around your ankles and you get saltwater in your ears, nose and eyeballs. I got smashed, and it was awesome.

Life isn't about playing it safe or staying between the lines. When you live by your heart, every day is a chance to experience life with enthusiasm and joy. Some days when I surf, I get dumped wave after wave. While the local pros are effortlessly duck-diving, I peg my board to the side, dive under the whitewash and get twisted in the ocean vortex. But I'm having so much fun because I set my intention to 'FUN'. And when I'm laughing, they are laughing too. Judgement doesn't exist in these experiences for me, just pure delight. I am grateful to be out there learning about the ocean, whirling in the sea's currents and experiencing the power and magic of nature.

Showing up with a positive intention is the key to having fun. Set an intention of 'fun' before doing your activities. Daily tasks can be sprinkled with joy. Cleaning the house? Listen to rock'n'roll and head bang at the same time. Studying? Make comedic moments out of your notes. Working? If possible in your job, play your favourite music. It's boring to be serious all the time. Be playful.

The Onward Journey

First of all, I want to say a huge thank you to *you*. Thank you for your support, trust and commitment. Thank you for following my journey and for believing in my book and my work. *You* are my inspiration. *You* are a warrior.

We may have reached the end of our road together in this book, but it's not goodbye. I will be with you each and every day on this adventure I call 'life'. I can't tell you that the road ahead will always be easy. But what I can tell you is that the moments that challenge us the most are often the moments where we grow the most. When life asks us to fight and we show up with presence, love and strength, we make breakthroughs. These breakthroughs are what change the way we see the world, the way we feel about ourselves, the way we think and the way we act.

Before you step out into the world, here are a few things I'd love for you to remember …

1. Be a compassionate friend to yourself.
2. Always ask questions and focus on your *why*.
3. Support yourself with healthy habits.
4. Embrace your authenticity.
5. Never give up on your dreams.

So, let's do it! You have everything you need to create the life you desire. It's up to you to begin. To make the *choice* to start.

This book is your superhero toolkit, here for you any time you need it. Are you ready to walk down the rainbow road of happiness, love and discovery? Yes, you are! Let me know how you go.

I'll be thinking of you!
It's your epic life.

Love, Iz

References

Page 9:
John Fayyad et al., 'The descriptive epidemiology of DSM-IV Adult ADHD in the World
Health Organization World Mental Health Surveys', *ADHD Attention Deficit and Hyperactivity
Disorders*, 19 November 2016, vol. 9 no. 1, pp. 47–65, doi.org/10.1007/s12402-016-0208-3
Edward Hallowell and John Ratey, *Delivered from Distraction*, New York: Ballantine Books, 2005

Page 22:
Philip M. Ullrich and Susan K. Lutgendorf, 'Journaling About Stressful Events: Effects of
Cognitive Processing and Emotional Expression', *The Society of Behavioural Medicine*, August
2002, vol. 24 no. 3, pp. 244–50, transformationalchange.pbworks.com/f/stressjournaling.pdf

Page 24:
Katie Dalebout, *Let It Out: A Journey Through Journaling*, Carlsbad: Hay House, 2016

Page 27:
Carol Dweck, *Mindset*, New York: Random House USA, 2006

Page 30:
Pema Chödrön, *When Things Fall Apart*, Boston: Shambhala Publications, 2005

Page 41:
The Work of Byron Katie, *The Work is a Practice*, thework.com/instruction-the-work-byron-
katie, 2021

Page 45:
Sophie H. Bennett et al., 'Rewiring the connectome: Evidence and effects', *Neuroscience & Biobehavioral
Reviews*, May 2018, vol. 88, pp. 51–62, ncbi.nlm.nih.gov/pmc/articles/PMC5903872

Page 47:
Svend Davanger et al., *Fighting Stress*, Oslo: Acem Publishing, 2008

Page 48:
Rich Muir, *The Meditation Spot*, themeditationspot.com.au, 2021

Page 60:
Swami Satchidananda, *The Yoga Sutras of Patañjali*, Virginia: Integral Yoga Publications, 2012

Page 81:
Fitness Australia, *Behaviour Change Strategies for Personal Trainers*, fitness.org.au/courses/
behaviour-change-strategies-for-personal-trainers/2551, 2020
George T. Doran et al., 'There's a S.M.A.R.T. Way to Write Management's Goals and
Objectives', *Management Review*, 1981, vol. 70, pp. 35–6, community.mis.temple.edu/
mis0855002fall2015/files/2015/10/S.M.A.R.T-Way-Management-Review.pdf

Page 104:
Marc David, *Nourishing Wisdom*, New York: Bell Tower, 1991

Page 110:
Lynette L. Craft and Frank M. Perna, 'The Benefits of Exercise for the Clinically
Depressed', *The Primary Care Companion to the Journal of Clinical Psychiatry*, 2004,
vol. 6 no. 3, pp. 104–11, ncbi.nlm.nih.gov/pmc/articles/PMC474733
Thomas M. DiLorenzo et al., 'Long-term effects of aerobic exercise on psychological
outcomes', *Preventitive Medicine*, January 1999, vol. 28 no. 1, pp. 75–85, sciencedirect.com/
science/article/abs/pii/S0091743598903851

Page 116:
Timothy W. Puetz et al., 'Effects of chronic exercise on feelings of energy and fatigue: a quantitative synthesis', *Psychological Bulletin*, 2006, vol. 132 no. 6, pp. 866–76, doi.org/10.1037/0033-2909.132.6.866
University of Georgia, 'Regular Exercise Plays A Consistent And Significant Role In Reducing Fatigue', *ScienceDaily*, 8 November 2006, sciencedaily.com/releases/2006/11/061101151005.htm
Ben Greenfield, *Boundless*, Auberry: Simon & Schuster, 2020

Page 126:
David T. Neal et al., 'Habits—A Repeat Performance', *Current Directions in Psychological Science*, 1 August 2006, vol. 15 no. 4, pp. 198–202, lescahiersdelinnovation.com/wp-content/uploads/2015/05/habits-Neal.Wood_.Quinn_.2006.pdf

Page 133:
Traci Mann, 'Why do dieters regain weight?', *Psychological Science Agenda*, May 2018, vol. 32 no. 5, apa.org/science/about/psa/2018/05/calorie-deprivation
Mercedes Sotos-Prieto et al., 'Association of Changes in Diet Quality with Total and Cause-Specific Mortality', *The New England Journal of Medicine*, 13 July 2017, vol. 377 no. 2, pp. 143–53, nejm.org/doi/pdf/10.1056/NEJMoa1613502?articleTools=true

Page 139:
Michael Pollan, *In Defense of Food*, New York: Avery Publishing Group, 2008

Page 140:
Mark Hyman, *Food: What the Heck Should I Eat?*, New York: Little, Brown & Company, 2018
Cleveland Clinic Health Essentials, *Which Is Worse for You: Fat or Sugar?*, health.clevelandclinic.org/which-is-worse-for-you-fat-or-sugar, 10 September 2019

Page 141:
Walter C. Willett and David S. Ludwig, 'Milk and Health', *The New England Journal of Medicine*, 13 February 2020, vol. 382 no. 7, pp. 644–54, takecarebr.com.br/wp-content/uploads/2020/03/MilkHealth_WillettLudwig_2020_Review.pdf
Kimberly Snyder, *The Beauty Detox Solution*, Ontario: Harlequin, 2011
T. Colin Campbell and Thomas M. Campbell, *The China Study*, Kent Town: Wakefield Press, 2007
The Doctor's Farmacy (podcast), 'Why Most Everything We Were Told About Dairy Is Wrong' with Dr David Ludwig, episode 131, 2020
Mark Hyman, *Food: What the Heck Should I Eat?*, New York: Little, Brown & Company, 2018
W.K. Arney and C.B. Pinnock, 'The Milk Mucus Belief: Sensations Associated with the Belief and Characteristics of Believers', *Appetite*, February 1993, vol. 20 no. 1, pp. 53–60
L. Ebringer et al., 'Beneficial Health Effects of Milk and Fermented Dairy Products – Review', *Folia Microbiologica*, 16 December 2008, vol. 53 no. 5, pp. 378–94, ssu.ac.ir/cms/fileadmin/user_upload/Mtahghighat/tfood/ARTICLES/milk/Beneficial_Health_Effects_of_Milk_and_Fermented.pdf

Page 146:
Richard F. Hurrell et al., 'Inhibition of non-haem iron absorption in man by polyphenolic-containing beverages', *British Journal of Nutrition*, 9 March 1999, vol. 81 no. 4, pp. 289–95, doi.org/10.1017/S0007114599000537

Page 150:
Samantha Olsen, 'McDonald's Hamburger Sits In Stomach Acid For Hours; Watch What Happens', *Medical Daily*, 31 July 2014, medicaldaily.com/mcdonalds-hamburger-sits-stomach-acid-hours-watch-what-happens-295988

Page 151:
Mark L. Dreher and Adrienne J. Davenport, 'Hass Avocado Composition and Potential Health Effects', *Critical Reviews in Food Science and Nutrition*, 2 May 2013, vol. 58 no. 7, pp. 738–50

Page 152:
C. Bosetti et al., 'Cruciferous vegetables and cancer risk in a network of case–control studies', *Annals of Oncology*, 2012, vol. 23 no. 8, pp. 2198–203
Ella Katz et al., 'Indole-3-carbinol: a plant hormone combatting cancer', *F1000 Research*, 2018, vol. 7 no. 1, pp. 1–9, ncbi.nlm.nih.gov/pmc/articles/PMC5989150

Page 153:
Mary P. Guerrera et al., 'Therapeutic Uses of Magnesium', *American Family Physician*, 15 July 2009, vol. 80 no. 2, pp. 157–62, aafp.org/afp/2009/0715/p157.html
Katharina Kessler and Olga Pivovarova-Ramich, 'Meal Timing, Aging, and Metabolic Health', *International Journal of Molecular Sciences*, 18 April 2019, vol. 20 no. 8, pp. 1–16
Antonio Paoli et al., 'The Influence of Meal Frequency and Timing on Health in Humans: The Role of Fasting', *Nutrients*, 28 March 2019, vol. 11 no. 4, pp. 1–19

Page 156:
Hrefna Palsdottir, 'Does Eating Fast Make You Gain More Weight?', *Healthline*, 14 June 2019. healthline.com/nutrition/eating-fast-causes-weight-gain

Page 157:
Gaia, *Secret of Water*, gaia.com/video/secret-water, 2015

Page 161:
Marc David, *The Psychology of Eating Podcast*, podcasts.apple.com/au/podcast/the-psychology-of-eating-podcast/id987724897, 2020

Page 175:
Erin E. Ayala et al., 'U.S. medical students who engage in self-care report less stress and higher quality of life', *BMC Medical Education*, 6 August 2018, vol. 18 no. 189, pp. 1–9, ncbi.nlm.nih.gov/pmc/articles/PMC6080382

Page 189:
Pema Chödrön, *When Things Fall Apart*, Boston: Shambhala Publications, 2005

Page 202:
Emmy Brunner, emmybrunner.com, 2021

Page 206:
Anthony L. Rostain and J. Russell Ramsay, 'A Combined Treatment Approach for Adults With ADHD–Results of an Open Study of 43 Patients', *Journal of Attention Disorders*, 1 November 2006, vol. 10 no. 2, pp. 150–9
Alex R. Kemper et al., 'Attention Deficit Hyperactivity Disorder: Diagnosis and Treatment in Children and Adolescents', *Comparative Effectiveness Review*, January 2018, no. 203, ncbi.nlm.nih.gov/books/NBK487761
Mark L. Wolraich et al., 'ADHD Diagnosis and Treatment Guidelines: A Historical Perspective', *Pediatrics*, 1 October 2019, vol. 144 no. 4, doi.org/10.1542/peds.2019-1682
Hsiang Huang, Heather Huang et al., 'Approach to Evaluating and Managing Adult Attention-Deficit/Hyperactivity Disorder in Primary Care', *Harvard Review of Psychiatry*, vol. 28 no. 2, pp. 100–106
J.J.S. Kooij, D. Bijlenga, L. Salerno et al., 'Updated European Consensus Statement on diagnosis and treatment of adult ADHD', *European Psychiatry*, February 2019, vol. 56 no. 1, pp. 14–34, pubmed.ncbi.nlm.nih.gov/30453134

Nora D. Volkow et al., 'Evaluating Dopamine Reward Pathway in ADHD: Clinical Implications', *Journal of the American Medical Association*, vol. 302 no. 10, pp. 1084–91, doi.org/10.1001/jama.2009.1308

John T. Mitchell et al., 'A Pilot Trial of Mindfulness Meditation Training for Attention-Deficit/Hyperactivity Disorder in Adulthood: Impact on Core Symptoms, Executive Functioning, and Emotion Dysregulation', *Journal of Attention Disorders*, November 2017, vol. 21 no. 13, pp. 1105–20, ncbi.nlm.nih.gov/pmc/articles/PMC4045650/pdf/nihms556138.pdf

Page 208:

Nathan Gallagher, *Breath By Nathan*, breathbynathan.com

Lloyd Lalande et al., 'Breathwork: An Additional Treatment Option for Depression and Anxiety?', *The Journal of Contemporary Psychotherapy*, June 2012, vol. 42, pp. 113–19, bjarnesand.se/wp-content/uploads/2020/01/An-additional-treatment-option-for-depression-and-anxiety.pdf

Page 210:

Matthijs Kox et al., 'Voluntary activation of the sympathetic nervous system and attenuation of the innate immune response in humans', *Proceedings of the National Academy of Sciences of the United States of America*, 20 May 2014, vol. 111 no. 20, pp. 7379–84, pnas.org/content/pnas/111/20/7379.full.pdf

Page 226:

Gabrielle Kassel, '17 Benefits Of Masturbation That Show Masturbating Is Good For You', *mindbodygreen*, 27 May 2020, mindbodygreen.com/0-18581/10-reasons-to-make-masturbation-part-of-your-wellness-routine.html

Page 230:

Thich Nhat Hanh, *How to Love*, Berkeley: Parallax Press, 2014

Page 233:

Gaétan Chevalier et al., 'Earthing: Health Implications of Reconnecting the Human Body to the Earth's Surface Electrons', *Journal of Environmental and Public Health*, 12 January 2012, vol. 2012 no. 291541, pp. 1–8, hindawi.com/journals/jeph/2012/291541

Page 239:

Gerd Gigerenzer, *Gut Feelings: The Intelligence of the Unconscious*, New York: Viking, 2007

Page 241:

Yasmin Boland, *Moonology*, London: Hay House, 2016

Page 249:

Jiunn-Horng Kang and Shih-Ching Chen, 'Effects of an irregular bedtime schedule on sleep quality, daytime sleepiness, and fatigue amont university students in Taiwan', *BMC Public Health*, 19 July 2009, vol. 9 no. 248, pp. 1–6, ncbi.nlm.nih.gov/pmc/articles/PMC2718885

AASM Sleep Education, 'Why you only need 7 hours of sleep', *Healthy Sleep Habits*, 3 June 2015, sleepeducation.org/why-you-only-need-7-hours-sleep

Jean-Philippe Chaput et al., 'Sleeping hours: what is the ideal number and how does age impact this?', *Nature and Science of Sleep*, 27 November 2018, vol. 10, pp. 421–30, ncbi.nlm.nih.gov/pmc/articles/PMC6267703

Page 257:

David Suzuki Foundation, *"The Dirty Dozen" cosmetic chemicals to avoid*, davidsuzuki.org/queen-of-green/dirty-dozen-cosmetic-chemicals-avoid, 2021

Acknowledgements

Writing a book feels like climbing a huge mountain ... multiple times. I'm grateful for all the support and encouragement from my team, partner and family. I want to thank the experts at Murdoch Books for believing in me and helping me bring this book to life. Thanks to Nathan Gallagher, Emmy Brummer, Rich Muir and Brittani Doherty for their invaluable help with this book. Thank you to my mum and Paul for always lending a helping hand and reading my work. To my beautiful managers and agents, thank you for always caring for me and supporting me. Benny, thank you for being by my side, cool as a cucumber, through many deadlines, listening to me ramble, believing in me and always putting time aside to help me with this book. Oh, and let's not forget my number-one dude, Bee. I couldn't have roadtripped in my campervan writing this book if I hadn't had you by my side; always ready to take my mind off things, give me cuddles and go on adventures. Most importantly, thank you to all of my followers, for supporting my work and encouraging the evolution of this book.

Love forever,
Isabelle